BETRAYED

BETRAYED

Stan Telchin

ZONDERVAN™

GRAND RAPIDS, MICHIGAN 49530 USA

ZONDERVAN™

Betrayed
Copyright © 1981 by Stan Telchin

First published in the USA in 1981 by Chosen Books

First published in Great Britain in 1982 by Marshall Morgan and Scott, a forerunner of Marshall Pickering

Requests for information should be addressed to:

Zondervan, *Grand Rapids, Michigan 49530*

Stan Telchin asserts the moral right to be identified as the author of this work.

A catalogue record for this book is available from the British Library

ISBN 0 551 00941 1

Scripture quotations from the *New Testament in Modern English* (Revised Edition), © J.B. Phillips 1958, 1960, 1972, are used by HarperCollins*Publishers*.

Scripture quotations identifed KJV are from the *King James Version* of the Bible.

Scripture quotations from the *American Standard Version* of the Bible © 1929, are used by permission of Thomas Nelson & Sons.

Quotations used in the Appendix regarding Prophecies and Fulfillment is taken from an article in SCIENCE SPEAKS by Peter W. Stoner, © 1962, Moody Press, and used by permission.

Printed and bound in the United Kingdom

03 04 05 06 /CLY/ 14 13 12 11 10 9 8 7 6 5 4 3

Dedication

For the glory of God.
For Ethel and Judy and Ann.
For believers who need to know.
For inquirers with hungry hearts.
For the curious.

Preface

Somewhere, tucked in among statements I heard while I was in college was this one: "Answers in life are a dime a dozen. Everybody has a better answer. The real problem in life is coming up with the right questions."

Searching for answers to the right questions can change your life. In the chapters which follow I'll share with you some of the questions I asked and the answers I discovered. They have dramatically changed my life.

Contents

Introduction

If I have learned one thing in my 35 years as both a magazine and book editor, it is to whiff out a good story as it comes by. What are the basic elements of a good story? Conflict, confrontation, suspense.

The first time I leafed through Stan Telchin's manuscript, I knew it had all the ingredients. The suspense begins when Stan, a 50-year-old Jewish insurance man, member of the Million Dollar Round Table, takes a tremulous phone call from his daughter, Judy. She has some startling news.

"Betrayed," is Stan's reaction when he has hung up the phone.

BETRAYED then became what we call a "search" book. It begins with Stan Telchin's determination to prove that his daughter, a Jewess, made a terrible mistake when she accepted Jesus as the Messiah. To do this he takes on Judy's challenge to read the Bible and find answers for himself. The discoveries Stan makes, leads him into a deeper quest to find the essense of his Jewishness. The climax comes when Stan, wife Ethel, and daughters Judy and Ann have a family confrontation over their faith and what it means to them.

This is not only a dramatic family story as it searches out its roots of faith, it also gives a fascinating account of what happened to the Jewish Christians in the early centuries. Why did so many leave the faith? Today the issue seems to be—can a Jew accept Jesus as the Messiah and remain Jewish?

In the process of editing BETRAYED I've gotten to know all the talented, creative members of the Telchin family and to value them as dear friends. In our tumultuous and confusing world I am convinced their story has special significance to people of all faiths.

Leonard E. LeSourd
Editor

1

The Telephone Call

The telephone call that completely turned around the lives of every member of my family came at 10:30 P.M. on a Sunday evening.

It was from our older daughter, Judy, age 21, a junior at Boston University. When the phone rang, my wife, Ethel, was in the shower. Ann, 17, our other daughter and a senior at Walt Whitman High School in Bethesda, Maryland, was in her room doing homework.

"Hi, Dad. It's Judy. Can you talk?"

"Sure I can talk, Jude. Everything okay?"

"I'm fine, Dad. But what I have to say is very important."

There was a strange edge to Judy's voice. Alarm bells rang inside me. Something was wrong.

"What is it, Judy? What's happened?"

"Now don't be alarmed, Dad. I'm okay. It's just that I've been wanting to talk to you all day. Can Mom get on the other phone?"

"Mom's taking a shower."

"Well, okay. You can tell her later."

"I'm listening, Jude."

"Dad, I've written you a very long letter. Spent days on it. I finished it this morning and have been reading and rereading it all day. But I can't mail it to you. I don't want it to hurt you. This is the hardest thing I've ever tried to do. I want to read the letter to you now. May I, Dad?"

I fought off a series of negative thoughts which raced through my mind: she was pregnant . . . she had run off and gotten married . . . she was in trouble with the police . . . she had been kicked out of school. But since Judy was such a wonderful daughter—so mature and sensible—none of these thoughts made any sense. I forced myself to remain calm.

"Jude, wait a minute before you start reading. Let me get paper and pencil so that I can make notes."

Ethel was still in the bathroom, so I picked up a pencil and note pad and went back to the phone to deal with Judy's news.

"I'm ready, Jude."

My daughter hesitated and then once again apologized for what she was about to tell me. She was now speaking quite rapidly and I could feel my own throat tighten in response to her anxiety.

My tension, I knew, was due to the fact that we were such a close-knit family, sharing openly the good and the bad. Ethel and I always have been proud of our daughters. Ann was a good student and showed an unusual gift in the field of art. Judy was majoring in special education at Boston University, training to work with handicapped children.

Judy had started out at the University of Maryland which was only a 30-minute drive from home. She had lived on campus in a busy dorm for a year and a half but felt too pressured. The following January she entered Boston University where she had taken a small apartment of her own. She had told us that things were going much better in Boston.

At this point in early spring 1975, I had never felt so on top of things. At age 50 I had a very successful life insurance business, a wonderful wife, two lovely daughters, a beautiful home. Everything in me was suddenly resistant to the upsetting news I knew was about to come from my daughter.

"Dear Mom and Dad," she began. "It's hard for me to write this letter because I love you and Ann so much. I never knew a family could be as close as we are . . . "

Numbly, I listened to Judy describe in detail all that she loved about our family life: how we as parents didn't preach one thing and do another, how real we were with each other, how she had loved growing up in a home of love and peace and how grateful she was for the way we had raised her.

Then as she went on to describe a recent period of loneliness my hand tightened on the phone. But she had solved the loneliness by taking a job on an emergency hot line where she was able to help people in need through the telephone. A long story followed about a man who had nearly committed suicide and how inadequate she had felt over the phone with him. But there were people working with her who had more experience and different points of view. They also had more answers than she did.

She then began to tell me about Dick. Dick was a "Bible believer," she said. He worked on the hot line too. They had become friends. Dick would talk to Judy about the Bible at length, and when Judy explained that she had never read the Bible and indeed did not own one, Dick brought her a Bible. Over the months Dick would then suggest things that she should read, and she would look them up.

"I had long talks with Dick, Dad, and from what I learned in those talks and read in the Bible and a whole lot of other things, too, well . . . "

I held my breath as she paused for composure.

"Well, I've become a believer too."

There was a long moment of silence.

"What does that mean, Judy?"

"It means that I believe in God. I believe that the Bible is the Word of God, and (long pause) I believe that Jesus is the Messiah!"

I was speechless.

Many parents might have welcomed Judy's words, but they absolutely crushed me!

You see, we are Jewish!

To mention the name of Jesus is awkward enough. To consider Him as the Messiah is something we just do not do. For any of us to believe that Jesus is the Messiah is to betray our people, to join the enemy and to desecrate the memory of all of our ancestors over the last 2,000 years.

How could Judy do this to us?

Rage started to well up within me. My first reaction was to blast her over the phone. The words were aimed when another voice welled up within me and said, *Don't retaliate. Keep the conversation open. Judy's been brainwashed. This is just a fad. She loves you and you love her. Don't let this conversation end in anger! Love her through this craziness and she will come to her senses.*

And that's what I did. Though I was dying inside, I kept the conversation open by asking questions, not passing judgment. "Look Jude," I finally said, "there is no way we can resolve this thing tonight. You're coming home for your spring break in a couple of weeks. I promise you that we will have lots of time to talk. You'll tell us more about it. For now let's just let things sit and cool off. Okay?"

I heard a sigh, there was a long pause, then a deep breath.

"Okay, Dad. I love you. Goodnight."

I put the phone down, absolutely drained.

Long before, Ethel had finished her shower. She had come into the den after Judy and I had been talking for about 10 minutes and heard most of my side of our conversation. When I hung up, she was very pale and very angry.

As I started to tell her Judy's side of our conversation, she suddenly jumped up and rushed into the kitchen. I could hear her talking to herself and banging pots around in frustration. Somehow I must go and try to calm her.

As I entered the kitchen, she stared at me with stricken eyes. "Where did we go wrong? Could any mother or father love a child more than we have loved Judy? How could she do this to us?"

Then Ethel began to cry. I can't stand to see my wife cry. In the 27 years of our marriage it had happened only on very rare occasions. Each time it really tore me up. Now my rage began to mount afresh as I saw I would be unable to take her hurt away.

In many ways, Judy's action was even worse for Ethel than it was for me. As close as my relationship was with Judy, Ethel's was even closer. If you have ever loved—really loved—and been loved in return, you will begin to understand the depth of that relationship. Ethel had invested herself completely in Judy and Ann. And this is how Judy paid her back. How do you cope with a child who turns her back—not only on you—but upon all her people?

There was little sleep in our home that night.

The next morning at my office I called a rabbi I knew and poured out over the phone the events of the previous night. His response eased the tension and provided hope.

"Whoa, Stan, slow down. It's not that terrible. Judy has had an emotional experience. But she's coming home in a couple of weeks, and you can deal with it face to face. She's a good Jewish girl. You love her. She loves you. She'll come to her senses. Just reason with her. It could be a lot worse, you know. She could be messed up with drugs or something. She's reaching out. She'll be all right."

With that assurance I relaxed a bit and called Ethel to

share his advice. He obviously had seen cases like this before and knew much better how to handle them than we did. Maybe by the time Judy came home, she'd be back to normal. What's the sense of worrying? *There's time enough for that later*, I told myself.

I did my best to concentrate on business for the next two weeks; then it was time to meet Judy at the airport.

2

What Happened to Judy?

As we drove to the airport Ethel and I planned our strategy.

"We need to act very calm," I said. "By now Judy will probably have come to her senses."

"What if she feels stronger than ever about it?" My wife asked.

"Then we'll use logic and reason with her. She'll see how wrong she is. But we must be relaxed and act as if nothing serious has happened."

The plane was late. I must have smoked half a pack of cigarettes as we waited.

When Judy walked through the gate, I blinked. Her face was alive, her figure trim as always. There was a vitality about her I had never seen before. She hugged us so lovingly I felt tears coming. I turned to get her luggage, not wanting her to see the emotion on my face.

During the 40-minute ride home we kept the conversation light, but when we settled down in the den the strain showed through our dialogue. I finally got to the point of concern. "Well, Judy, I guess it's time for us to talk. We need to know what's been happening to you. Do you want to tell us?"

"Yes, Dad, I really do."

As she said this, Ann appeared from her room and joined us. The contrast between the two girls suddenly troubled me. Judy, sitting on the sofa, was nervously exuberant, her large hazel eyes alive with color, her hands moving constantly to give expression to her words. Ann sat motionless, curled up in a corner of our L-shaped couch, her eyes somber and disapproving, her face pale and set. She had reacted more angrily to Judy's news than either Ethel or me, probably because she felt deserted and left out. The girls had always been so close. It actually hurt me on the inside to think that they might be separated over this matter. Judy just had to see what she was doing to our family.

Ethel sat on the sofa next to Judy, her face a blend of emotions: love and motherly tenderness, disapproval, confusion.

Avoiding a direct confrontation, I asked Judy to tell us again in detail what had happened.

"Being alone in my small apartment gave me a chance to think, really think for the first time in my life," she began. "I discovered that I wasn't happy with myself. Aside from you guys, my life was almost meaningless. Most of the kids I knew were messed up in one way or the other. For the first time in my life I felt a need to get in touch with myself and to reach out to others." She paused. Tensely I reached for a cigarette.

"That's why I took that job at the hot line," she continued.

"Explain that to us, Judy."

"Well the organization is called 'Project Place.' It's a crisis intervention center. People call in by phone with all kinds of special needs and problems, and we try to help them."

"Is it Christian?"

"No. It's not connected with any organization. They have an ambulance, a small, paid staff, some volunteers."

"What do you do there?"

"I handle a phone. Answer questions if I can. Refer questions to specialists if I can't. I was working the night shift when Ronnie's call came in."

"Who's Ronnie?" my wife asked.

"I didn't know him before he called. When I answered the phone, he gave his name, said he was a veteran and that he didn't want to live any longer. He said he had just swallowed 52 Seconal tablets."

"What did you do?" I asked.

"I nearly panicked. I asked him where he lived, told him we would send an ambulance to get him to the hospital. He refused at first. I begged and begged for an address. Finally, he gave it to me. Then I did something that was against the rules."

"What was that?"

"The ambulance and driver weren't available, so I convinced another man on duty that we should go in his car to take Ronnie to the hospital."

"Why was that wrong?"

"Only qualified medical people should handle such cases. If we had gotten him into the car and he had died, we could have been held responsible."

"That makes sense."

"It does and it doesn't. If we had waited for the ambulance, it would have been too late. As it was we got Ronnie to the hospital barely in time. They had a terrible time saving him."

Impatiently, I cleared my throat. "In your telephone call you told me about Ronnie and his brother Charles. What are they to you?"

"Just friends. But before I tell you about Charles, I want to tell you about Dick."

I could see by the tears welling up in her eyes that the tension of the situation was getting to Judy. I decided not to interrupt if I could help it and just let her tell her story.

Again she told of her relationship to Dick, the man she worked with who had such a special love for the Jewish people and who had given her a Bible to read. "He really loved the Bible and would come to me all excited about something he had read and tell me to be sure to look it up. I would make a note of the verses and read them when I got home. But I really didn't understand what he was excited about. It was very frustrating. I kept on reading, though, and trying to understand."

Then as Judy began to talk about Ronnie again, she turned to Ann, "You remember the night I talked to Ronnie? You were visiting me in Boston and sat with me as I worked the phones. You took over the phone and talked to Ronnie while we left to get him. Remember?"

Ann nodded her head but said nothing.

"Well, they saved Ronnie, and he kept asking for me to come to visit him. I did go to see him a few times while he was in the hospital, but I couldn't get through to him. I couldn't relate to where he was coming from. I would talk to him about love, but he would talk to me about hate. It was like we were in two different worlds."

As she spoke, Judy's face revealed the empathy she felt.

"I felt so bad for him. He was so mixed up. He needed help so badly, but I couldn't provide it. Then he was released from the hospital. A few weeks later he took another overdose of pills and was rushed back to the hospital. When I heard about it, I went to see Dick and asked him to pray for Ronnie. And Dick did a strange thing."

"What was that," Ethel asked.

"He took me aside, gave me this stern, fatherly look and said, 'Forget Ronnie for a moment. What about you?' I didn't know what he meant and said so. Dick then got out his Bible and read a passage that said, in effect, why look at the mote that is in your brother's eye and not see instead the beam that is in your own? As usual, I didn't understand what he meant, so he explained that I was too concerned about Ronnie and not concerned enough about myself."

"What did he mean by that?" I asked.

"He meant that I was so busy trying to help others that I didn't recognize my own needs. He said that I was the one who should pray for Ronnie but that I should begin by seeking God for myself. He said this to me very gently, but nevertheless it set me thinking. I spent the whole next day—alone—in my apartment. I read some of the Bible. I thought about God. Finally I tried to talk to God. Then I began to cry."

At this point Judy's voice broke. Her eyes filled with tears as she struggled for composure. Ethel started to put her hand out to Judy, but I noticed that she pulled it back.

What is going on here? I thought.

"I couldn't stop crying—for hours, I guess," Judy continued. "It was the strangest experience of my life. The tears just kept coming, and I kept calling out to God for help. I asked Him to reveal Himself to me and to show me the truth. I was confused and upset. In my heart I was beginning to believe some of the things I had read in the Bible and what Dick had been telling me about the Messiah, but my head kept saying 'This is impossible! You can't believe this! You're Jewish. You can't believe in Jesus.' I cried for hours and finally fell asleep."

When Judy regained her composure she continued.

"The next day I knew that something had happened to me, but I didn't understand what it was. I was numb, and my eyes were all red from crying. You know how that sometimes happens to me. But I just had to pull myself together. You see, I had an appointment with Charles."

"Ronnie's brother?"

"Right. I had met Charles once in Ronnie's hospital room. He had just gotten out of prison after a long sentence, and I was terrified of him. He is a huge man with

tatoos on his arms. I fantasized that he was part of the Mafia
or something and that he must have been the one to get
Ronnie into trouble in the first place. Well, Charles had
called me on the hot line one day to ask me if I would help
him get Ronnie admitted to the VA hospital in Bedford,
Massachusetts. They have a good drug rehab program. He
asked me to go there with him to see one of the admissions
people."

"You didn't do it, did you?"

"I didn't want to, of course. As I started to say no, I suddenly heard myself say yes. Then I made an appointment to
meet him a few days later."

When we all shook our heads, Judy laughed and said, "I
know you think I've lost my mind, but let me tell you what
happened. He asked me to meet him at his mother's house;
I'd met her once in the hospital. As soon as I arrived there,
Charles led me to his car. Reluctantly I got into the front
seat and sat as near the door as I could. As we headed for
the VA hospital, I saw something on the front ledge of the
car that surprised me—a black book. It was a Bible."

I just sat there, looking at her in dismay. Why had she
forgotten my instructions for handling situations like this?

"I asked Charles if that was his Bible, and he said it was,"
she continued. "And then something strange happened. I
knew that I was safe with him. And so I relaxed, and we
began to talk. Since I had asked about the Bible, he began to
talk about it. All of a sudden I found myself asking him a
question I never planned to ask him. I said that a friend of
mine had told me that even though I'm Jewish I can believe
in Jesus. So I asked him if that was true."

His answer was that Jesus was Jewish and that many
thousands of Jewish men and women believed in Him
when He lived on earth. Then Charles started to talk to me
about how Jesus had come into his life while he was in solitary confinement. It's an astounding story. He was put into

solitary confinement because he was full of hate, and they couldn't manage him. But while he was there he accidently took a Bible from the bookmobile and read it. It changed his life. He came out of solitary a new man—full of love. Even got his marriage straightened out."

I didn't want to hear any more about Charles. "What about Ronnie?" I asked.

"We had our interview at the hospital and were able to get him into the program. On the way home, Charles told me that the best thing I could do for Ronnie was to pray for him. Later, when we reached my car, Charles invited me to join him and his wife at his church the next Sunday. I thanked him, but said no. That's the last thing I felt I needed.

"In the weeks that followed, Charles would call me every few days to tell me what was happening with Ronnie. This one day he again asked me to join them at church. Maybe it was curiosity, but I said that I would. It was very strange, so different from our synagogue. But the people got to me. They were so loving, so welcoming, so reassuring. They had so much joy. At the end of every service, the pastor invited people to come forward to be saved."

"To become Christians," I clarified. "They want you to stop being a Jew and become a Christian."

"No, Dad, that's not the way they explained it. They said I would be returning to the God of Abraham, Isaac and Jacob. I would be returning to the God of my fathers."

"So that's how they do it!" Ethel said.

"How many times did you go to that church?" I asked.

"Three times," Judy replied. "The first two times I just watched the people and listened to the service, trying to understand. No one pressured me. I was accepted. They really cared for me. Back at my apartment I would try to read the Bible and think about what it said. I made the decision about Jesus when I was all by myself on Saturday

night. After I made it, I couldn't wait to get to the church
the next morning. I didn't even hear the pastor's sermon.
All I could think about was that when he asked the question
about who wanted to receive Jesus as Lord, I was going to
raise my hand. That's just what happened. Then he asked
me to come forward so that he could pray with me."

There was a long, uncomfortable silence in our den as we
tried to absorb the meaning and significance of Judy's
words.

"But Judy, you're Jewish," I said softly. "Jews just don't
believe in Jesus. How can you be Jewish and believe in
Jesus? It's impossible!"

"Oh, Daddy, you're wrong. You'd be surprised at how
many Jews there are today who believe in Jesus."

"Baloney."

Judy looked about the room and saw the disappointment
in everybody's eyes. She sighed. "Look, Dad, you have just
got to find out more about this. You don't have to believe
what I believe or believe me, but you're an intelligent man.
Read the Bible for yourself and find out whether it's true or
not. All of you do it. It's either true or it's false. If He isn't
the Messiah, you'll know it. And if He is, you'll know it. But
read the Bible for yourselves and come to your own conclusions."

With that we closed the discussion and went to bed.
Ethel seemed too numb to talk about it. She just kept shaking her head. I turned out the light and tried to sleep, but
sleep for both of us was far away. Silently we turned and
tossed.

"What are we going to do?" Ethel finally asked.

"I think I'll do what she asked me to do."

"What do you mean?"

"Judy wants me to read the Bible. Okay. That's what I'll
do. And when I read it I'll be able to prove to her that she is
absolutely wrong. In fact, I'll bet that's just what she wants

me to do."

"I don't know," Ethel sighed. "She seems very sure of herself."

"It's an act."

There was silence for a few moments.

"Stan . . ."

"What, dear?"

"Judy really looks good, doesn't she?"

"Yes, she does."

"Do you think all this joy and sparkle is because of her new beliefs?"

"Possibly," I said impatiently. "She's happy now because she's made some new friends. But it won't last. She's Jewish. Nothing can change that. She won't find lasting happiness with Christians!"

"I guess you're right."

I knew I was right. And I couldn't wait to begin reading the Bible to prove it.

3

Family Heritage

Why was I so upset? Because I know the story of my people!

My mother and father were from a little ghetto town in Russia called Stullen. Anyone who saw *Fiddler on the Roof* would recognize Stullen. My parents faced all the hardships Tevya's family faced in "Fiddler" and many more. The terror of the pogroms, the vicious attacks upon the Jewish people, all of it put a fear in their hearts which was never removed. The people who did these things to the Jews were the "Christians." And we believed that anyone who wasn't a Jew automatically was a Christian.

My dad came to the States in 1904 with my grandfather and several of my uncles, not knowing when he left that my mother was pregnant. Two years later they had earned enough money to bring over the rest of the family. Then my father met his son for the very first time. The son's name in Jewish was Zelig Hirch. In English, he would be called Charles.

My parents settled on the East Side of New York where Pop was a tailor, just like the guy in "Fiddler." Learning English was a tremendous problem for them all and getting used to American ways was difficult, but as the years went by they made their adjustments.

The years brought more children. First there was Joe, next came Frances, then Sam. A break of 10 years followed, then Dorris was born. Two years later came the final surprise when I entered the world.

I don't remember too much about those very early years of my life, but I do remember when I was called a "Christ killer" for the first time. I couldn't have been any more than five or six. I rushed home crying, not because I understood what a "Christ killer" was, but because I was afraid of the hate I heard in the voice.

Later, when I was eight, I was playing ball in the school yard on a Sunday in July. All I had on was a pair of shorts and my sneakers. As I started home for lunch, I encountered a big, grim-faced woman coming down the street. She stepped directly in my path and with the side of her right arm shoved me across my chest and knocked me down saying, "Out of my way, ya little kike!"

Again that anger—that hate which I could not understand. And I began to cry. I rushed home to my mother, and she quieted me and soothed my tears. That's when Mom started to tell me about what it was like to grow up in the ghetto and about the hatred that the Gentiles had for Jews.

Over the years that followed, I learned about the knights of the Crusades who descended on Jews with a cross in one hand and a sword in the other. They murdered and raped and pillaged, all in the name of "Christianity."

Then there was the Inquisition in Spain in 1492, when refusing to convert to Christianity would cost a Jew his life. The watchword of the day must have been, "The only good Jews are converted Jews or dead Jews."

I learned about the Maranos. These were the Spanish Jews who converted to Catholicism publicly in order to save their lives and those of their families. But in the privacy of their homes they maintained their identity as Jews and taught their children about Jewish life.

Meanwhile our family had moved from the ghetto on the East Side of New York to a ghetto in Williamsburg, and finally to a ghetto in Borough Park, Brooklyn, New York, where our neighborhood was 40 percent Jewish, 40 percent Catholic and 20 percent everybody else. But all of my real friends were Jewish. I remember that we used to have street fights when the gangs from 37th Street or from 8th Avenue would set out to "get the Jews" and descend onto our territory on 43rd Street. We lived on a block which was made up of apartment houses from corner to corner and from side to side. There were hundreds of kids on the block. My buddies were Big Hy, Little Hy, Sid and Al. All of our parents were from Russia or Poland, and we had a particular attraction and respect for one another.

What I remember most vividly about those gang fights was that no matter how much I hated Benny or Sol from the building next door, we would forget our differences, link arms and defend ourselves against our common enemy, the "goyim" (the Hebrew word for Gentiles).

I was a Jew because I was born a Jew. As far as I was concerned there was no other way that one could become a Jew and, short of death, there was no way that one could stop being a Jew.

All of my relatives on both sides were orthodox Jews. While in Russia, their lives had been intertwined with the ghetto, religious schooling and synagogue life. But that is not the way it was for us in America. For us, Judaism, the formal religious part of being a Jew, was rarely discussed or even considered. My three brothers and I were all trained for our Bar Mitzvah and that was that. There was nothing else to do except "be."

I tried to develop the discipline of putting on my tvillin (phylacteries*)[1] each morning because I knew that this would be pleasing to my grandfather. These were small leather boxes containing portions of the Scripture and were worn on the left arm and around the forehead. He had given me the tvillin his grandfather had given him for his Bar Mitzvah, and to please him it was very important that I continue to follow this practice. But I didn't understand why we Jews had to do it, even if it was in the Bible. No one else was doing it. My father didn't. My brothers didn't. Why did I have to? So I gave the tvillin back to my grandfather. I knew that he was hurt, but I didn't want to get stuck with having to do this for the rest of my life, and I didn't want to lie to him. I remember how Grandpa looked at me, shrugged his shoulders, sighed and then took them back.

My grandfather went to the synagogue twice a day and was highly respected there, but my father and brothers and I rarely went. The formal religious part of being a Jew did not seem relevant to us. I could read a little Hebrew carried over from my Bar Mitzvah days, and I knew the major prayers, but their recital was form without content to me. I had almost no concept of the God of Abraham, Issac and Jacob. I did occasionally say a prayer when I was in trouble or pain, but I never knew the meaning of answered prayer or believed that my prayers were even heard.

But I enjoyed being a Jew. I enjoyed the holidays and the food and the Jewish language which is so expressive. Sometimes it is impossible to find words in English which do justice to the Jewish idiom.

Some of my fondest memories have to do with the Jewish holidays: the solemnity of Rosh Hashanah and Yom Kippur; the joy of Passover; the presents of Channukah. Of them all I suppose that I enjoy Passover most. I remember how we used to celebrate it at my grandparents' home. During Passover, we ate only unleavened bread to commemorate the Exodus from Egypt when our ancestors were fleeing and could not wait for leavened bread to rise. Everything that had to do with leaven was removed from our home. The dishes, pots, glassware, silverware, everything would be changed. Then Grandma would go to work in the kitchen. By the time we were seated at the table, her face would shine as she beamed her love and approval at the 16 or 20 of us who would be gathered to celebrate the Seder, the reading of the Hagaddah which told of the exodus of the Jewish people when God delivered them from out of bondage.

My chief interests were Jewish life, Jewish causes and Jewish organizations. I joined a Zionist youth group when I was 12 and stayed in it until I was 15. I walked the subways of New York, collecting money for the Jewish National Fund. I went to rallies and discussion groups.

When I went into the army in February 1943 at the age of 18, it was much the same. I would occasionally go to services to be with other Jewish guys, and I'd go for the high holidays. But God wasn't involved in our services or our conversation. I don't remember any of my buddies talking about God. My cynical attitude of the time went like this: I mean, really—with all that is going on in Germany, do you expect me to believe there is a God? That we are his "Chosen People"? Chosen for what? The gas chambers? *Do me a favor*, I thought, *choose someone else for a change!*

I met Ethel David when we were both in Montauk Junior High School. Since I was a year older, we had little in common except that we both worked as reporters for the school paper and were both musicians. Ethel played the flute, and I played the trumpet. The fact that Ethel was friendly with several of the girls in our crowd occasionally brought us together.

I routinely invited Ethel to my Bar Mitzvah as a part of our gang, but Ethel did not include me in her sweet 16 party. This annoyed me. I crashed the party which made Ethel angry. She would have asked me to leave if her sister Bess hadn't stopped her.

After that I paid very little attention to Ethel until World War II broke out. I was home on furlough just before going overseas when I ran into Ethel at a friend's house. She surprised me with her charm and sophistication; her hair was piled way up on top of her head; she had on a good-looking suit, high platform shoes, good makeup. I asked Ethel if I could walk her home. We talked for more than an hour as we stood in front of her house. Lonely and on edge about what was going to happen overseas, I was quick to accept her offer to write to me.

For the next year and a half Ethel was not only a great letter writer, but she was remarkably creative in the packages of goodies she sent. When the war was over and I returned home after three-and-a-half years in service, the first thing I did was to walk over to her house. It was a Saturday night. I rang the front door bell and waited. Her mother opened the door and said, "Come in, son." How prophetic!

But Ethel wasn't at home. She was working in a specialty store on Fifth Avenue in Brooklyn. To kill some time I walked the eight blocks to the store.

When I entered the shop, Ethel was waiting on a customer. I stood there for a moment, staring at her, thinking again how sharp she looked. When she saw me, her face lit up, and something pinged inside me. After she finished work we talked for a long time, and I made a date to see her the next day in Prospect Park where she was going horseback riding.

The next morning I arrived at the riding stables in my GI uniform since it was all I had. Ethel appeared wearing a light brown jacket, dark riding pants and high brown boots. She looked stunning as she tied her horse to the hitching post. I felt like a klutz.

With a warm smile Ethel took my hand and led me to a black and white horse nearby. As soon as I approached, the animal began to snort and shuffle his feet.

"Frisky, isn't he?" I said, trying to cover up my dismay. The truth was, I was not a good rider.

"He'll be all right once you mount him," Ethel said, eying me carefully.

"Hmmm." I studied the horse for a few moments. "He seems bothered by me; maybe it's the uniform. Let's talk a while until he calms down."

Ethel nodded, and we sat down on a nearby bench. As we talked, once again I found Ethel to be intelligent, articulate, positive, confident and very feminine. She was also perceptive. An hour or so later, sensing I didn't want to go riding, she suggested we return my unfriendly horse to the stable.

I quickly agreed. Ethel turned in both horses. I insisted on paying the fees and happily followed her to a park bench where we could continue our conversation.

By the time I went off to George Washington University a few months later, we had become quite serious about each other. Our romance had its ups and downs over the next two years, but we were in love and knew that we would marry. At the end of my junior year, I began looking for an apartment as a prelude to a September wedding. Those were the days when with millions of GI's being discharged from the service, good apartments were treasures. When I found one on P Street, in northwest Washington, D.C., I called her in wild excitement. "Why wait until September? Let's get married now." Three weeks later the semester ended, and three days after that, on May 26, 1948, Ethel David became Mrs. Stanley S. Telchin.

After receiving my bachelor's degree in drama from George Washington University, I went to Catholic University for my master's. Just prior to graduation I was asked to join Player's Incorporated, the university's graduate touring company, to play Macbeth in *Macbeth* and Leonato in *Much Ado About Nothing*.

Ethel was asked to join the company as wardrobe mistress and stage manager. We toured 29 states and Canada for nine months, visiting more than 122 cities. At the end of the tour, heady with our success, Ethel and I headed for New York City to try our fortune on Broadway.

Tough times followed. Soon it was necessary for Ethel to take a job as a buyer at Stern's Department Store. I sought roles for several more months before accepting a position selling ties in a fashionable mens' store. From here I moved to a job with the United Jewish Appeal of Greater New York.

By June 1952 Ethel and I knew that our future did not lie in theatre or in New York. We returned to Washington, D.C., where I began work for the State of Israel bond program, under Harry Brager. Out of this came the discovery that I had a real ability for public relations. When Harry started his own public relations firm, he asked me to join him as an account executive. For the next two years I traveled extensively as we handled campaigns for Brandeis University, the B'nai Brith, and other Jewish organizations.

It was during this period that Judy was born, and we bought our first home. When it became obvious that traveling four days a week was no way to build a family life, I switched into the life insurance business. Ann was born two years later in 1957. By this time my new career was flourishing.

As the years continued and our family relationships developed, I was careful to enroll our children in religious schools. Judy continued her Jewish studies until her confirmation, just before she was 16. Ann had her Bas Mitzvah just before she was 13. The girls learned a lot about the

Jewish people and our history, but they knew very little about the Torah or about God. There was little discussion of either in the Reform Congregation, which we attended, or in our home. Social issues? Yes. Jewish causes? Yes. But God? I'm afraid not. We could not give to the girls what we did not have.

In time I became a Chartered Life Underwriter and a life member of "The Million Dollar Round Table." Our home in Bethesda was a large, L-shaped rambler, with swimming pool and magnificent landscaping. Inside there was a huge modern kitchen, formal living room, dining room, spacious den, four bedrooms, four bathrooms. There was an office, game room and spacious recreation room in the basement.

My work within the Jewish community had earned me a "Man of the Year" award for one organization, election to the board of directors of another and trusteeship of two others. I was recognized as a solid member of the Jewish establishment.

Then Judy dropped her bomb!

4

The Search Begins

Sunday night Ethel and I put Judy on the 7:30 plane to Boston. As we drove home in our new BMW Bavaria we were silent. I listened to the hum of the engine. The longer our silence, the louder the hum grew. Silence is not natural with us, though I must say that normally conversation flows more easily from Ethel than it does from me. But this Sunday night we were both lost in our thoughts.

I was thinking about the changes which had taken place in Judy. Just six months earlier, Judy had informed us she didn't want to go to our synagogue to celebrate the Rosh Hashanah service. I insisted that she go. Pouting, Judy had dressed in one of her shorter dashiki's and had put on makeup with a look which was definitely not one of my favorites: heavy, white eye-coloring with heavy black outlines, and skin devoid of all color. As conservatively dressed as Ethel and Ann and I were, Judy's get-up stuck out glaringly.

But the Judy that we had just been with didn't look anything like the Judy of last fall. She wasn't wearing any makeup, but her eyes shone with enthusiasm and conviction, and her skin glowed with good health. She wore skirts and blouses and dresses, like the civilian garb of my background, instead of the extreme attire of the "now" generation. She was also a lot calmer than we had remembered her, despite the strain of confrontations with us.

While I was deeply involved in my thoughts, Ethel asked a very simple question. "Stan, what are we going to do about Judy?"

"Get her back. I'll read the Scriptures as I promised. There will be the ammunition I need to disprove what Judy has come to believe."

"How long will it take?"

"I think I can read the Bible in 10 or 12 hours, maybe four or five nights. If I need help, I'll get it from the rabbi."

When we got home, I began to gather the material I thought I would need. I was surprised at how much was available. First I dug out my copy of the Soncino edition of the Torah. I knew I would need it to counteract the various other Bibles Judy had given to me. I had a pocket-sized New Testament which highlighted fulfilled Messianic prophecies and gave Old Testament references, as well as the King James and American Standard Versions. I set these up near my chair in the den and gathered together some legal pads and sharp pencils. I was too tired to begin that Sunday night but was determined to begin the very next night.

On Monday I rushed home from work. After dinner I directed a determined look at Ethel and left the kitchen for the den. One additional preparation: a good supply of cigarettes.

Ensconced in my favorite chair, I lit a cigarette and reached for the Prophecy edition of the Bible. This was going to be my first reading of the New Testament, and I didn't know what to expect. I was a bit apprehensive and mentally girded myself for a book of hatred against the Jewish people. After all, how else could you possibly explain the last 2,000 years?

I opened the book and read this inscription pasted on the

front page:

> In appreciation of the gift of this Book, I will read it
> and will pray to God to show me the Truth as I
> read.

SUGGESTIONS

1. Read one or more chapters in the book each
   day.
2. Ask God to show you the truth as you read.
3. Look up the references to the Old Testament.
4. Carry the book in your pocket whenever possible.

The inscription startled me for a moment. *Who put it
there?* I wondered.

On the next page I read this:

> O God of Abraham, Isaac, and Jacob, show me the
> truth as I read this book; and help me to follow the
> light that is given me by Thee. Amen.

Below were several lines of Hebrew, obviously a translation of the prayer I had just read. It felt strange to read these
instructions and see this prayer in a Christian book. More
quickly I turned the next few pages and began to read the
book of Matthew.

My first stop came in chapter one where the virgin birth
of Jesus is described. Noting a reference back to Isaiah 7:14,
I picked up my copy of the Soncino edition of the Torah and
tried to find it. Not there. But it was in the King James version: *Therefore the Lord himself shall give you a sign: behold, a
virgin shall conceive, and bear a son, and shall call his name Im-
manuel.*

I'd always thought that this particular verse, which I had
seen on Christmas cards for years, was from the New Testament. What a shock to find it in the old!

The concept of Jesus being born of a virgin was so incomprehensible that I put it aside to consider later.

When chapter four introduced the devil, I began to squirm with discomfort. I certainly did not believe in devils and had always felt sorry for people who did.

Later in this chapter there was a reference to Deuteronomy 6:13. I looked it up: *Thou shalt fear the Lord thy God, and serve him, and shalt swear by his name. Ye shall not go after other gods, of the gods of the people which are round about you; for the Lord thy God is a jealous God among you, lest the anger of the Lord thy God be kindled against thee, and destroy thee from off the face of the earth.*

Wow, I thought. *That's heavy. Is that what Judy did? Is that what I have to bring her back from doing?* Then my eye moved across the page and I saw: *Hear, O Israel: the Lord our God is one Lord.*[1]

The Shema! The cornerstone of my faith. The watchword of the Jewish people. Our God is one. There is only one God. How could Judy fall into the trap of thinking that there are three gods and believing in them? I made a note on my pad to discuss the virgin birth and the trinity with someone who could give me more information about them.

But as I was writing my notes, my mind went back to the verse I had just read in Matthew. Jesus had said, "Begone, Satan! For it is written, you shall worship the Lord your God, and serve Him only."[2] Jesus himself was saying that there was only one God! I put my pad down, picked up the Bible and continued to read.

Several chapters later, in Matthew 15, I was suddenly riveted to a story about a Gentile woman who came up to Jesus and asked Him for help. He replied by telling her that he had not been sent to help her but to help *the lost sheep of the house of Israel.*[3] I was stunned at this because I again realized how very little I knew about this man. And yet he had come, he said, to help the Jewish people.

At this point, I put down the little Prophecy edition I had

been reading and picked up the larger King James Version of the Bible. I opened it to chapter 16 of Matthew and began reading. At verse 13 I noted Jesus' question: "Whom do men say that I the son of man am?" And Simon Peter answered and said, "Thou art the Messiah, the Son of the Living God." Jesus replied: "Blessed art thou, Simon Bar-jonah: for flesh and blood hath not revealed it unto thee, but my Father which is in heaven."

Again, I had to stop and ponder: *Who do men say that he is? And who do I say that he is? Could he be the Messiah? Could God possibly have had a son?*

I made some notes on my pad as I reduced these questions to writing, then for the rest of the evening concentrated on what I was reading. Maybe it was because of my love for the theatre and knowledge of Elizabethan English or maybe because of my Jewish background, but I could visualize most of the scenes, the people and the situations which were developing before my eyes in the King James translation.

Three hours later I finished Matthew and a pack of cigarettes. I leaned my head back on my chair, closed my eyes and reflected on the totality of what I had just read. I had been prepared to read an anti-semitic book—a book of hatred against the Jewish people. A book filled with poison and with lies. But instead I found a very serious book written by a Jew to other Jews, about the God of Abraham, Isaac and Jacob and about a man referred to as the Messiah of Israel.

Not at all what I had expected.

After I finished, I went into the kitchen to join Ethel for a cup of tea. She looked at me quizzically.

"I've made a good beginning," I replied.

"How far did you get?"

"Through the book of Matthew."

"Is it bad . . . I mean, anti-semitic?"

I paused, trying to summarize my thoughts. "No, there's nothing anti-semitic about it. It's the story of this man, Jesus, what He does and what He says."

"No ammunition to disprove what Judy believes?"

"Not yet. But I've only started. I've gotten a good overview."

"How do you feel about what you've read?"

I looked at Ethel blankly. "What do you mean?"

"I mean, was what you read at all convincing?"

I shook my head vigorously and stiffened my inner thinking, pumping myself full of adrenalin against all that Judy had accepted. "When I get further into the book, I'll find what I need. Then we'll have no problem winning Judy back."

The next day while driving to my office, my mind churned with thoughts. *How can Judy do this to us? Haven't we given her everything?* She had been raised in a beautiful home, sent to the best schools, all her needs and wants provided. Our Jewish heritage was beautiful. How could she turn her back on it?

It took me only 15 minutes to drive from our Bethesda home to my office on Connecticut Avenue in Washington, D.C. My office was on the fifth floor, facing west, on what the younger agents called "The Gold Coast" because of the number of multimillion dollar agents officed on this side of the building. No sooner had I arrived than I knew I had to talk to George.

George was a Gentile colleague of mine in the insurance agency. We were friendly competitors but not really friends. About a year earlier he had become a Christian. I knew that he had been an Episcopalian and couldn't understand what he meant when he said that he had become a

Christian. I not only hadn't wanted to ask him questions about this but had wanted to avoid him because he had become one of those over-zealous Christians. He wanted to talk to everyone about his faith and was always giving out books and tracts and cassette tapes.

If you happened to have a backache one day, he would order you to sit down while he prayed over your feet so they would even up or something. Once when Ethel had hurt her back and was laid up, George asked if he could come to our home and lay hands on Ethel. I didn't know what he was talking about and gave him an ungracious reply that went something like this: "Look George, I know that you mean well. But I can't really tell you what would happen if you laid your hands on Ethel. All I know is what will happen if you lay even one hand on her! Buzz off, will you?"

That exchange had created a bit of a rift between us, but nevertheless I knew that I had to talk to George since he was the only Christian I knew with whom I could discuss Judy. Besides, George had calmed down a lot recently.

When I reached his office, George was talking on the phone. He motioned for me to come in and sit down. I did so. A moment later he hung up and greeted me. I tried to make small talk for a moment but couldn't manage it. Finally, I unloaded.

"My daughter Judy believes in Jesus."

"Praise the . . . " George stopped in mid-sentence, checking his obvious delight at the news. He looked at me carefully. "You're very upset about it, aren't you?"

"Yes, George, I am. To be blunt, Ethel and I feel betrayed by our own flesh and blood."

A look of warm sympathy crossed George's face. He got up from behind the desk, walked around to the front door which he closed, then he pulled over a chair and sat down next to me. "Let's talk about it."

I felt a bit trapped but told him the whole story. George is
an open man, and the expressions on his face shifted from
curiosity, to intense interest and then back to warm concern.

"I can feel your pain, Stan. How can I help you?"

"I'm not really sure, George. I'm not even sure why I
came in to see you this morning, since I have resented your
efforts to convert me from Judaism to Christianity."

"I don't want to convert you to my faith," he replied
quickly. "I respect your Jewishness. But I would like to see
you come to believe in Jesus as the Messiah. I know lots of
Jews who believe in Jesus. They are still Jews."

"How can that be?"

"Let me try to explain it to you this way. Jews and Gentiles are always going to be different—different backgrounds, culture, customs, way of life. Not all Gentiles are
believers in Jesus. To become a believer—whether you are
Jewish or Gentile—you have to come into a personal relationship with Jesus. In your terms, you have to receive him
as your Messiah. Believing this changes your entire life, but
it doesn't stop you from being a Jew."

I shook my head slowly, not knowing what to say.

"Here, Stan, let me give you some books on this subject.
These were written by guys just like you who have faced
similar problems."

"No! No, thank you, George. I don't want any more
books."

George looked at me intently then nodded. "If there is
anything I can do to help, please let me know."

That evening I plunged into the Book of Mark. I started to
read it in the Prophecy edition, but because the type was so
small, I decided to switch Bibles and began to read from the
American Standard Version. This was easier for two
reasons: first, the print was larger, and the language was
more up to date; second, every time the word Christ was

used there was a note over in the margin which said "i.e. the Messiah." Christ was a word that I had a terrible time hearing or saying except as part of an expletive. It just stuck in my throat.

All during my growing up years I had heard the name "Christ" many times, and always negatively. I really didn't want to know any more about him. But "the Messiah"— that was something else. I wanted to know everything I could possibly find out about Him! Seeing the reference to the Messiah in the American Standard made reading on a lot easier for me.

On Tuesday evening I finished Mark. On Wednesday, I finished Luke. My pad was filling up with notes, and I was continually going back to the Old Testament. Soon, I decided that I could not depend on the Gentile version of the Old Testament.

I went to a Jewish book store and bought a copy of the Tenach, the Jewish Bible. Complete and unabridged. I began to use it to check on the Old Testament references and found that it was almost exactly like the King James Version. There were only minor word differences.

On Thursday night, I tackled the Book of John and was fascinated by it. I read it slowly as I visualized the scenes it portrayed. By Friday night I had finished John and reflected on the first four books of the New Testament. I couldn't figure out why these four men each had to write his own version of what had happened. But at least I had finished the assignment. Now to disprove it.

I stared at my legal pad for what could have been hours. There were lots of questions on the pad. But what did they add up to?

Ethel was waiting for me in the kitchen, coffee ready. "How did you do?" she asked.

I poured myself a cup and sipped the black liquid reflectively. "I've finished the first four books. They tell the same story, but each tells it differently. The Book of John is the best written."

"I thought so, too."

I looked at Ethel sharply. "You've been reading the Bible?"

She nodded. "I have to find out for myself."

I sighed. "I suppose you must. Have you discovered anything in your reading that could help us with Judy?"

"Not really."

"What was your reaction?"

"About the same as yours. This Jesus was a good man, but if his claims for himself were not accepted by the Jewish leaders of his time and all the rabbis since then, why should we accept him?"

"You're right, Eth. We must point this out to Judy."

This exchange made me more determined than ever to find the answers I was seeking. For something had happened to me that first week.

The issue of "what Judy had come to believe" was being pushed into the background. Another issue was now clearly before me. The question had become personal. I needed to know the truth.

5

Heidi

It's time to introduce Heidi. In April 1969 she had become
our housekeeper and was now almost a member of our
family. Her real name is Heyde Carneiro Martins de Souza.
Since that's quite a mouthful, we call her Heidi. She is tall,
dark, attractive and intelligent and comes from Recife, Brazil.

Shortly before Ann's Bas Mitzvah in the Spring of 1969,
we had gone through a whole assortment of housekeepers,
none right for us, and were becoming desperate. Expecting
150 people for a reception following Ann's Bas Mitzvah in
June, Ethel had inquired of our neighbors and their maids
to see if they had any suggestions.

One neighbor told us about a woman she had met who
had recently come from Brazil and who might be available
for a short period of time. A meeting was arranged with
Heidi. Ethel discovered that she had an excellent education, was from a good family in Recife, Brazil, had come to
the States as a lark to learn English while employed as a
housekeeper in California and was now visiting a cousin in
Washington before returning to her own country. Ethel
asked Heidi if she would be willing to help us out through
June and Ann's Bas Mitzvah. Heidi agreed.

With that, a romance started between Heidi and our entire family. Ann's Bas Mitzvah went beautifully, and Heidi helped make it a success. She agreed to stay on after the Bas Mitzvah and was with us for more than nine years.

When Heidi told us that she was a Baptist, I couldn't help wondering how hard it must be to be a Baptist in a Catholic country. But she never talked about it unless we asked questions. She loved us and we loved her. After Judy's traumatic visit I overheard a rather significant conversation between Heidi and Ann in the kitchen one day.

"I think what Judy's done is terrible," Ann stated bluntly.

"It's a shock, and I feel for all of you."

"Why would she do it?"

"I think she felt a deep yearning for God," said Heidi quietly.

"But we believe in God."

"I know. But Judy wanted more than a belief in God."

"What do you mean?"

"She wanted to know Him as a person."

Ann was silent for a moment. "I feel like I've lost my very best friend." Ann was near tears.

"Try to see from Judy's side." Heidi put her arm around Ann. "She has found something that fills her with joy. Her face is more alive, lovelier than I've ever seen it. If she's happy, why can't you be happy for her?"

"Oh, Heidi! You just don't understand," Ann said. As she turned from Heidi she saw me and rushed into my arms crying. When the tears subsided, Ann took my handkerchief, dried her eyes and blew her nose.

"Oh, Daddy," she continued, "I feel so deserted. Judy was my very best friend in the whole world. I learned so much from her. All my friends were jealous of our relationship. But now she's deserted me. And I don't know how to get to her. She's so different. She looks different. She sounds different. When I try to make conversation with

her, that's all it is—just conversation. Daddy, what are we
going to do?"

Tears welled up in my own eyes as I tried to comfort Ann.
I just had to get to Judy. She had to be made to see what her
craziness was doing to our entire family. She had to stop
this Jesus business!

In my voluminous notes on the four gospels I had starred
the virgin birth of Jesus as being totally "off the wall." How
could Joseph have gone along with that nonsense?

One night while pondering this in the den, my mind
flashed back to 1949 and an incident that occurred while I
was a graduate student at the Catholic University of America. I never really thought I would get my master's degree at
a Catholic University and would not have if courses had
been required in theology or Catholic philosophy or Latin
or Greek. But the only required "Catholic" course was
called "Moral Aspects of Art and Literature." And that never hurt anyone, I thought, and so I enrolled.

In the Spring of 1950, I played the role of Friar Lawrence
in the drama department's production of *Romeo and Juliet*. It
was a wonderful production and drew much critical
acclaim. But the incident I recalled didn't occur onstage, but
backstage. Louis Camutti, a fine actor and a good Catholic,
was cast in the role of Benvolio. As I recall we only had one
major scene together. This was the tomb scene of Act five
when Romeo commits suicide because he thinks that Juliet
is dead.

During this long scene, Lou and I would be waiting on
the top of a large staircase so that, on cue, we could make
our descent into the tomb. While we waited, we would talk
about all sorts of things. On this particular night, Louis began to talk to me about the virgin birth. I heard him out and
then said something brilliant like this:

"Come on Louis! I've got a lot of respect for you and for what you believe, but do you really believe that stuff about a virgin birth? How can you believe that? You're not stupid. You know the facts of life. How can you believe that stuff?"

Louis looked at me very seriously and said, "I believe because I have the gift of faith."

"Well I don't," I countered, "I don't have that gift."

And that was the end of that. Louis never again brought up the subject, and I felt that my logic had overcome his superstitious faith.

I again focused on the scripture passages before me and thought, *Boy! If Louis could see me now!*

That thought made me so uncomfortable I stamped out my cigarette and headed for the kitchen to fortify myself with a cup of coffee. I found Heidi there and unloaded my skepticism on her.

"Heidi, do you consider yourself to be a good Christian?"

She shook her head. "I can only work at it."

"But you do believe in Jesus?"

"Yes."

"Do you also believe in the virgin birth?"

Heidi was thoughtful. "Yes. It makes complete sense to me."

"How can you say that?"

"For the Son of God to come to earth in any usual way would be, well, not like God. Jesus was too special. So God, Himself picked an innocent girl and planted in her body the seed that was to be Jesus."

I couldn't help a slight snort. "Why would God want to go through all that? Why wouldn't He just send Jesus down to earth as a man to do what he's supposed to do?"

Heidi had been putting the dirty lunch dishes in the dishwasher. She didn't answer right away, and I saw that her eyes were troubled. "I'm sorry, Mr. Telchin, but I have only a small knowledge of the deep things of God. When I don't understand something, I just put it aside for a time and trust that He will bring me understanding if He wants me to have it."

I went back to my den thinking that Heidi was like so many Christians who accept certain principles of faith simply because they were told to do so by some pastor or priest. Yet I found myself warming to her honesty and her openness. What she said came out as clear as mountain water flowing over white rocks.

Ethel and Heidi were also having almost daily conversations along the same line. Poor Heidi. She was getting a barrage of angry questions from all three of us. But I don't think I ever saw her upset; her love and compassion for us seemed inexhaustible.

After reading and analyzing the four gospels in the New Testament, I worked through my notes and came up with five basic questions I felt had to be resolved.

1. Do I believe that God really exists?
2. Do I believe that the Jewish Bible (The Tenach) is the divinely inspired word of God?
3. Does this Bible prophesy about a coming Messiah?
4. Is Jesus the Messiah?
5. If he is, what does that do to me?

I read and reread the questions with a growing sense of apprehension. I was on a quest all right, something that could keep me going for weeks, maybe months. Where would I find the time?

No sooner had I asked that question than I knew that time wasn't the problem. A lot of my work at the office could be turned over to my very capable secretary, Jenny Bignell.

For in my mind and heart I had come to one inescapable conclusion. Finding the answers to these questions was the most important work of my life.

6

What Do I Believe?

The first question to be answered was, "Do I Believe in God?"

This was not a theoretical question. There was to be no more of my ducking behind the philosophies of great men of biology or botany. Darwin was entitled to his vote, but that wasn't being asked for now. I had posed a question of myself. *I* had to answer.

As I pondered the matter, I remembered all the material I had read which set out to prove that anyone who believed in a "supreme creator" had to have at least one major screw loose. Every discovery which pointed to the fact that the earth might be billions of years old contained within it the accusation that the God of the Bible was a figment of man's imagination.

Over and over again when I was growing up, I remembered hearing the thesis expounded that "God was a creation of man's mind." Man created God in his own image, the argument raged, because man could not face the reality of life.

And so it went: "God is man's escape." "Religion is for cattle and Catholics." These and other supposedly smart sayings were designed to raise the speaker above the herd and let the world know that here was a man who could stand on his own feet and not have to look to anyone or anything for support. Here was a complete man who knew that this life is all there is and was warning everyone, "Make the best of this life because you'll never get out of it alive."

As I sat in my den and pondered the subject, I suddenly realized that I knew what a lot of others had said about God, but I had never really tried to articulate what I felt about God. Nor could I remember ever having discussed this subject with anyone: not my parents, brothers, sisters or friends—not even with Ethel. For some reason, this was a subject we didn't get into. And so while hearing about God all of my life, no one ever cajoled or pushed me to make a decision concerning my belief in God.

Yet at times I have called out to God. One such occasion occurred when I was about seven years old. We were living in the Williamsburg section of Brooklyn then, in a four-story apartment house at 375 Pulaski Street. There was a vacant lot next door, and most of the kids would gather there to play. One fall day a group of men came to tar the roof of our apartment house, and they set up their gear on our vacant lot. They built a fire and periodically heated up buckets of tar which they would then hoist up to the roof by a rope.

On this particular day, after the men had left the lot, we discovered that they had left behind a bucket of tar. It was still cooking on the fire. Benjy, one of the bigger kids, got a broom handle and told us to gather around. He forced the broom under the handle of the pail and called to me to grab the other end. Since he was older, I obeyed. I picked up my end of the broom and together we lifted the pail of tar and started to walk away. The tar was heavy, and as we walked, the bucket started to slide down the handle towards me. Well, you can picture what happened. The closer the bucket got to me the heavier it became. Then I felt the heat.

"It's too heavy!" I shouted.

"Hold on, kid," he snapped.

But it was too much for me. I dropped my end of the handle and the bucket fell to the ground pouring hot tar all over my legs. The pain was terrible. As I shrieked in agony, the other kids stared at me helplessly.

Finally two of the guys picked me up to take me home. As they were lifting me, I remember calling out to God: "God, how could You let this happen? What did I do? Please take away the pain!"

But the terrible pain persisted, and I was in bed for weeks with bad third-degree burns. My conclusions: Either God did not hear my prayers, or maybe there is no God.

So began a long period of doubt. And indifference. I found that something kept me from going all the way to atheism. Possibly it was the devoutness of my mother who lit candles every Friday night and then prayed earnestly to God, or my grandparents who struggled so hard to keep the family going to synagogue and practicing Jewish customs.

When I was in high school the theory of evolution really confused me. Then I concluded that to believe in evolution you had to reject belief in the God who called Moses to lead the "chosen people" into the promised land. To abandon belief in this God meant to abandon the very basis of the Jewish people. I couldn't do that. So I put the whole subject out of my mind.

Now, years later, I had to decide—did I believe in God or not?

As I sat there surrounded by my books and yellow pads, the enormity of this question hit me. For awhile, rebellion surged inside. Why should I believe in a God who ignored a small boy's prayer for relief from pain? Or who would let His people suffer so much persecution over the years, or allow six million Jews to be slaughtered in Nazi Germany?

But a sense of fairness deep within me made me look at the other side and see that God (or some power) had been good to our family, protected us during World War II and given our people a homeland in Israel after the war. It hadn't been all bad for all Jews.

And suddenly my rebellion crumbled. Deep in my heart I knew that I believed in God. I always had—inside. I didn't know how it all played out or what the effect of this decision would be, but I knew that God was. How or why He chose the Jewish people, how He could have allowed to happen to them what did happen to them was more than I could understand. But that wasn't the question at this particular moment. I *did* believe that God, by whatever name or form or power or force, really did exist.

That decision led me squarely to the next question: Do I believe that the Bible is the divinely inspired Word of God? Or do I believe that the Bible is merely the story of the Jewish people?

As I look back upon it now, I realize how critical the answer to that question was.

I leaned back in my chair to think about it. As I did so, I recalled an incident which occurred 20 years before. When Judy was one year old, we purchased our first house. As a new home owner and father, I thought that it was finally time for me to assert myself spiritually. Since there was a large conservative synagogue just a few blocks from our home, just before Rosh Hashanah in 1955, I filled out a membership card for our family and made a pledge to the building fund, all without ever having attended a service in the synagogue.

A week later, after the first night of the holiday, I knew I had made a mistake. While the rabbi probably was a fine man away from the pulpit, he had a tongue like a cat-o'-

nine-tails when he addressed the congregation. He was
whipping everybody. That took care of that. I was not
about to be whipped by anyone. Even more quickly than I
had decided to join the congregation, I decided to unjoin.

For the next few months we went to different congrega-
tions, including our first Reform Congregation. The rabbi
there was young and dynamic. Though this synagogue
didn't have the warmth and ritual which I remembered
from my youth, the services were almost entirely in English. I figured that what I would lose in nostalgia I would
make up in understanding.

And I liked the way he put things. The first time I ever
heard the rabbi speak, he had this to say:

"Some people will come to temple because they are lonely or because they are looking for business or looking for
understanding or looking for a husband or a wife or for
their identity. I don't care why you come, but come. And
let's pray and let's hope that together we will find God."

This was my kind of guy. He was intelligent and inquisi-
tive. And he hadn't found God yet either! So there was
hope for me.

In order to get a better fix on where Judaism was really at,
I decided to take the rabbi's first course in comparative religion. The first Monday night we met, there were about 12
people in the class. The rabbi asked a crucial question. It is
so crucial that I have never forgotten it.

"If all memory of organized religion were suddenly to be
obliterated from the face of the earth overnight—no more
synagogues, no more churches, or Bibles, or prayer-
books—what would happen?"

We thought about this for awhile, then someone offered
that without any form of religion we would have chaos.
There would be no basis for law or contracts or marriage
and so forth. Then later on, people would begin to ask
questions: Where did I come from? Where did you come

from? Who created the universe? Is there a God? How do I communicate with Him—or He with me?

The rabbi pointed out that while these same questions would be asked all over the world in time, different people throughout the world would come up with different answers. And that's the way it should be!

"Everyone is entitled to his opinion, right?"

And every head in the room went up and down. "Right. That's the way it should be."

And with that as a base, the rabbi led us in a study of comparative religions.

It had been 20 years since I took this course, but not until I posed the five questions to myself in the quiet of my den did I realize how unfair the rabbi's basic thesis was. He had laid a false foundation. He established the basic premise that no memory of organized religion existed when it certainly did. The memory of organized religion had not been obliterated from the face of the earth. Very much available was the record of all that God had done. Throughout time the Jewish people have been known as "People of the Book." Why did we know so little about that "Book" today?

I headed for the kitchen hoping I would find Ethel there. She was. "What now?" she asked as she poured me yet another cup of coffee.

"I can't believe I'm 50 years old and know so little about the Bible."

"You're making up for lost time, aren't you?"

"Sure I am. But it hurts to think that in all these years never once do I remember discussing the Tenach with anyone else—parents, brothers, sisters, friends, even rabbis. All I ever read was the prayer book. Who took the Bible away from us? How come I don't know more about it?"

Ethel and I looked at each other silently. There was no answer. Then I turned and went back to my den.

When I was seated, I took my yellow pad and tried to

record everything I felt about the Bible. There was our trip to Israel in 1973 when Tzvika, our guide, had been so enthusiastic concerning the archaeological discoveries being made in Israel. I remembered him saying that throughout Israel archaeological digs were continually unearthing discoveries which proved the authenticity of the Scriptures. He was so proud of what he termed "the Bible coming alive before our very eyes!"

More recently I had learned that the Bible had been translated into Greek about 250 B.C. but that the earliest Hebrew manuscripts were dated about 916 A.D. There was nothing to tie them together until 1948 when the Dead Sea scrolls were discovered. Scientists had reported that these scrolls had been written about 100 B.C. and were an extremely important link in determining the accuracy of the Scriptures and verifying each translation.

I noted that the scrolls of Isaiah were the most complete of the Dead Sea scrolls and that this was the book which contained the most Messianic prophecies. When the scientists compared Isaish 53 they found that out of the 166 words of the text, only one word of three letters was in question, and this word did not have any real consequence on the meaning of the text.

Over a period of weeks I concluded that what I had read about the Bible confirmed its historic accuracy. What remained to be determined was whether or not I believed that the Scriptures were divinely inspired or were merely an accurate record of past events.

For days I wrestled with this. One night I put the question to myself this way on my yellow pad: "Is it easier for me to believe that the Bible is just a story of the Jewish people or to believe that the Scriptures were divinely inspired?" From deep within me the answer came. *It is easier for me to believe that God inspired the writing of the Bible.*

I had answered the second question.

Now for question three. Does the Bible (The Tenach) prophesy about a coming Messiah?

By this time I had met a lot of believers through the books they wrote. Some were Jewish, but most were Gentiles. There were several books on prophecy which forced me to consider for the first time the prophecies contained in the Old Testament—a subject I had never before explored.

In the days that followed I discussed some of these prophecies with a few of the believers I had met. They kept pointing out other specific prophecies contained in The Tenach about the coming Messiah, prophecies which I had never before considered.

I read them with growing fascination. They told how the Messiah would come. Where he would be born. Under what circumstances. What he would do. How people would react to him. How he would die. When he would die. What would happen after he died.

In my continuing study of the prophecies, it became clear to me that the Messiah would have to be of the seed of David. There was no disagreement on this point from anyone I had ever met.

I was checking a prophecy one day in the Book of Daniel when these verses leaped out at me:

> Seventy weeks are determined upon thy people and upon thy holy city . . . to make reconciliation for iniquity, and to bring in everlasting righteousness . . . Know therefore and understand that from the going forth of the commandment to restore and to build Jerusalem unto the Messiah, the Prince, shall be seven weeks, and threescore and two weeks: the street shall be built again . . . And after threescore and two weeks shall Messiah be cut off, but not for himself: and the people of the prince that shall come shall destroy the city and the sanctuary.[1]

Intrigued but confused I took the verses to a mature believer who explained that 70 weeks of years referred to 490 years (70 times 7). Then he gave me a study which plotted the period beginning with the year of the restoration and rebuilding of Jerusalem. After making allowances for the difference between the lunar and the solar calendars, they came dangerously close to the years Jesus walked the earth.

The balance of that verse was interesting too. It talked about the Messiah being "cut off" and the city and the sanctuary being destroyed by "the Prince that shall come." Could this have occurred in the year 70 A.D. when Titus destroyed the Temple and the City of Jerusalem?

This prophecy really set my head spinning. If the Messiah had to prove that he was of the seed of David in order to be recognized as the Messiah, and if the Temple containing all of the genealogies had been destroyed, wouldn't it be impossible for anyone in the future to ever prove that he was the Messiah? This question left me with some alternatives.

Either the entire concept of a Messiah in Jewish life was a myth, and the Bible was false, or the Messiah came before the year 70 A.D.!

7

The Search Continues

To deal with the questions on prophecies about the Messiah, I had begun to do some outside research. This meant talking to rabbis, seeking out Jewish and Gentile writers and scholars.

In mid-May Ethel and I attended a benefit performance of *The Dybuk* in a Washington theatre. This is an old and fascinating movie about spirit life in Judaism. A local rabbi had organized the performance for his congregation and had agreed to chair a discussion group on the Sunday following the film.

The formal part of the rabbi's discussion involved a brief study of demons and spirits in Jewish literature. When he was finished, I raised my hand and asked if he would please discuss the concept of the "soul" in Jewish life.

The rabbi looked a little surprised and then said, "What's a soul?"

Everybody laughed.

By the time the laughter subsided, he had recovered his composure and said, "If by soul you mean the essence of a person, the *je ne sais quoi* that makes each person unique from all others, my answer will be very brief: I do not know. I do not know what makes us different on this level, apart from our genetic makeup, heredity and environment."

With that, the rabbi moved on to the next question.

A few moments later, I raised my hand again and asked the rabbi, "Will you please tell us about the Messiah?"

"What's a Messiah?" he responded.

Again the audience broke up in laughter.

By this time, I knew better than to continue to explore these subjects in this forum. After the meeting was over I approached him. We chatted for a moment, and then I told him how disappointed I was in his replies to my questions, that I really wanted to know more about the soul and the Messiah.

The Rabbi looked at me intently for a moment and then said, "Tell me, what makes you think I have the answers?"

"But you are a rabbi."

He shook his head. "The longer I live it seems like the less I know. In fact I probably have even more questions than you do."

I was stunned at his response, though disarmed by his candor.

How could a graduate of one of the major conservative seminaries in the country make such a statement? If *he* didn't know the answers, how could I know them?

At this period it seemed as if I had mostly questions. When I was a little boy during the depression and asked my family to buy me something they could not afford, why did they say, "You will get it when the Messiah comes"? Why, when the Jewish people were being destroyed in the concentration camps of Germany, did many people in the synagogue say, "It will soon be time for the Messiah to come"?

What is a Messiah anyway?

I searched through important books: *A History of the Jews*, *Jews, God and History*, and *My People*, but none of these supplied the information I was seeking. I delved into Gerson Scholem's *The Messianic Idea in Judaism*, until I discovered that he was writing from a humanistic point of view.

Then I found Joseph Klausner's *The Messianic Idea in Israel*, and with great anticipation began studying. In the author's treatment of the concept of the Messiah as being a person, he exited me with this statement:

". . . the prophetic hope for the end of this age, is one in which a strong redeemer, by his power and his spirit, will bring complete redemption, political and spiritual, to the people of Israel and along with this, earthly bliss and moral perfection to the entire human race."

But as I read on my frustration mounted. Through some 500 pages Klausner describes what different men have said about the prophecies contained in Scripture and how these opinions have been argued back and forth over the centuries. Some argued for a messanic person, others for a messanic age. But while the arguments raged on, one fact remained unchanging: "The messianic idea is the most glistening jewel in the glorious crown of Judaism."

If this statement was true, how was it possible that almost no one in Jewish life was speaking about the Messiah today?

How is it possible that one could even say in jest, "What's a Messiah?"

Why is so little written on the subject?

Why could I not find anyone to discuss this subject with me who is not either embarrassed or anxious during the discussion?

Has the dream of the Jewish people been only a dream after all?

Have we run out of theories?

My frustration was intense because I had been searching the Scriptures and considering the Biblical prophecies on the one hand, while on the other I had been reading of the conflicting opinions of men. When I compared their theories, written over the centuries, with the question raised by John the Baptist, they were completely unsatisfying.

John had sent a messenger to Jesus to ask this question: "Are you he that should come? Or look we for another?"

If no person to be known as the Messiah was expected, how could John have asked that question? And Jesus gave this answer: "Go your way and tell John what things ye have seen and heard: how that the blind see, the lame walk, the lepers are cleansed, the deaf hear, the dead are raised, to the poor the gospel is preached."[1]

The reality of the question and the power of the reply had more impact upon me than all the various theories reported in Klausner's book written hundreds of years later.

In such a manner did my days of study and questioning continue. By this time I had almost completely left my business. Jenny, my secretary, was instructed to do the very best she could do without me and to call me only if she really needed me. I had a job to do at home.

I now worked in my den from early morning until late at night. While I had smoked a little more than a pack a day for years, I was now smoking more than two packs of cigarettes a day. My eyes were rimmed with red, and I was aware of Ethel's concern as she watched me when we talked. I also knew that she watched me while I worked.

During this period, my conversation with others had become fairly one-dimensional. If they could add insight into the study I was doing, I wanted to talk with them about it. I had little patience for small talk. In the beginning, as I discovered new elements, I would come to Ethel and ask her if she knew this or had come across that. And I would discuss how I felt about what I was reading and discovering.

One day I realized that this had to stop. Because of our

deep love for one another, we continually wanted to please each other. But this issue was too important for that. So we made a pact: Ethel would continue with her study as I would continue with mine. We would try not to influence one another. We would just trust, and hope that we would both come to the same conclusion when our studies were completed.

As I sought answers, I made discoveries. One was Beth Messiah, a congregation of Jewish and Gentile believers located in Rockville, Maryland. I remember my reaction when I first heard of this group. I couldn't believe my ears. I had to see it. Sure enough, it was true; there were Jews and Gentiles worshipping together at a Friday night service. There I met Jewish men and women of all ages and backgrounds who labeled themselves "believers." They also called themselves Messianic Jews and spoke glowingly about "Yeshua Ha Mashiach," a term I had never heard before but which I was told was the translation in Hebrew of Jesus, the Messiah.

One night at Beth Messiah one of the men told me of a conversation he had had with a pastor some years before:

"Tell me, young man," the pastor said, "what do you think of Jesus?"

"To tell you the truth, I don't."

"You don't what?"

"Think of Jesus."

"Why is that?"

"Because I'm Jewish."

Pause. "Do you think Jesus could be the Messiah?"

"No, I don't!"

"Why not?"

"I told you, I'm Jewish."

"Tell me, have you ever read the New Testament?"

"No, I haven't."

"Have you ever read the Old Testament?"

"No, not really."

"Well, young man, let me see if I understand you. You have never read the Old Testament. You have never read the New Testament. But you are convinced that Jesus is not the Messiah. Is that right?"

"Right!"

"You certainly form definite conclusions on no evidence, don't you?"

Ouch! That dialogue hit me in the gut, because that's where I was before Judy came home with her bombshell.

One of the non-Jewish couples we met a few Friday nights later, Dick and Meg, over a time became very good friends of ours. They not only had a sincere love for the Jewish people, they also knew a great deal about the Bible. After our first meeting at Beth Messiah, they invited Ethel and me to go out with them for coffee. At a nearby restaurant we explained what had happened with Judy and what we were going through. They in turn shared some of their experiences, and we all felt a strong pulling to get to know one another better.

We learned that Dick had a fine job on Capitol Hill as an attorney, while Meg spent a great deal of her time teaching Bible classes. They had two beautiful children and a lovely home.

As we began to meet in each other's homes, Ethel and I were relieved that they never pushed or tried to force us to accept their views. Instead they patiently answered our questions and referred us to the Bible for more information.

One night as we were leaving their house, Meg said to me, "You know, Stan, I think that you really need to study three specific passages about prophecy—Jeremiah 31:31, Isaiah 53 and Psalm 22."

I wrote the passages down and told Meg that I would read them when I got home. Later that evening I went into the den and looked up the Scriptures Meg had suggested I study. The first was Jeremiah 31:

> Behold, the days come, saith the Lord, that I will make a new covenant with the house of Israel, and with the house of Judah.
>
> Not according to the covenant that I made with their fathers in the day that I took them by the hand to bring them out of the land of Egypt; which my covenant they broke. . . .
>
> But this shall be the covenant that I shall make with the house of Israel. After those days saith the Lord, I will put my law in their hearts; and will be their God and they shall be my people.

I could hardly believe what I was reading. A *new* covenant? Was God saying He would no longer be remembered as the God who brought us out of the land of Egypt? How could that be? It was in the Exodus and in the giving of the Law that we received our definable substance as God's *chosen people.*

Was a time really coming when God would no longer be remembered as the God who did these things? When would that time be? Why had I never seen this before? Why had we never talked about this in my home or in the synagogue?

I rushed from the den into the bedroom to share the verses with Ethel. But I was too late. She was already in bed asleep. I returned to the den and found the 53rd chapter of Isaiah. Beginning with the third verse, I was gripped by a new discovery:

> He is despised and rejected of men, a man of sorrows, and acquainted with grief: and we hid as it were our faces from Him; he was despised and we esteemed him not . . .
>
> But He was wounded for our transgressions, He was bruised for our iniquities: the chastisement of our peace was upon Him: and with His stripes we are healed . . .

> He was oppressed, and he was afflicted, yet he
> opened not his mouth; he is brought as a lamb to the
> slaughter, and as a sheep before her shearers is dumb,
> so he openeth not his mouth . . .

Was not this an exact description of the Jesus whom I had
read about in the New Testament but written hundreds of
years before his birth?

Then I read these verses of Psalm 22, written more than
500 years before the crucifixion of Jesus:

> My God, my God, why hast thou forsaken me? Why
> art thou so far from helping me, from the words of my
> groaning? . . .
>
> All who see me mock at me, they make mouths at
> me, they wag their heads; he committed his cause to
> the Lord; let him deliver him, let him rescue him, for he
> delights in him! . . .
>
> My strength is dried up like a potsherd, and my ton-
> gue cleaves to my jaws; thou dost lay me in the dust of
> death.
>
> Yea, dogs are round about me; a company of evil-
> doers encircle me; they have pierced my hands and
> feet—
>
> I can count all my bones—they stare and gloat over
> me;
>
> They divide my garments among them, and for my
> raiment they cast lots.

While reading I could see a man hanging on a tree. The
prophecies were becoming clearer and clearer to me.

There was little sleep for me that night. I stayed in the
den thinking until well after 2 A.M., and I knew my answer
to question number three: The Tenach *does* contain in-
numerable prophecies concerning a coming Messiah.

Then more questions rushed in. 'Does Jesus of Nazareth
fulfill these prophecies? Is Jesus the Messiah?'

Everything within me strained at these two questions.

All of my secular Jewish identity said: "Don't answer them! Remember the Crusades. Remember the Inquisition. Remember the pogroms. Remember the things which have been done to the Jewish people in the name of Christ for the last 2,000 years."

8

The Covenant Relationship

During this period of inner upheaval, we continued to have our regular telephone conversations with Judy. But they weren't the same. We did our best to keep our conversations light and newsworthy. We didn't tell her what we were really going through, but we knew that she knew.

The most difficult relationship was between Judy and Ann. Before Judy's change, they had been extremely close. It was hard to believe that they were four years apart in age. They had so much in common, always telling each other jokes and stories and laughing and kidding around with each other. But now it was different. Ann didn't even want to talk with Judy on the phone. Every time we tried to discuss the situation with Ann, she would just get up from the table or a chair in the den and run into her room, eyes brimming with tears.

When Judy would call and ask to talk to her, Ann would shake her head and mutter a lame excuse. And those few times when Ann picked up the phone at Judy's call, she would speak in short, chopped sentences and then turn the phone over to one of us as quickly as she could.

And it was hard for me too. I couldn't very well encourage Judy when I was being torn up on the inside. And I couldn't share with her what I was doing. All that I could do was to love her and trust that this would all work out. Often when Ethel and Judy were on the phone talking and Judy would ask for me, I would signal Ethel that I just wasn't ready to talk with Judy. Then Ethel would make an almost transparent excuse that I was busy or just on my way out and late for an appointment.

Every time one of these incidents occurred I became more and more determined to finish my analysis of the Bible so that I could convince Judy how wrong she was. But it was turning into a much more difficult project than I ever expected. In fact, it had become a mission of the highest order.

One morning I decided to go to my office and handle certain matters. But once there I couldn't do any work—no concentration. In exasperation I got up from my desk, closed the office door, and reached for my Bible. That was the morning I came across the passage in John which so jolted me:

> Do not think that I will accuse you to the Father: there is one that accuseth you, even Moses, in whom ye trust. For had ye believed Moses, ye would have believed me: for he wrote of me.[1]

I was suddenly convicted anew of the fact that I didn't even know my own Bible, The Tenach, much less anything about the Christian Bible. *Admit it, Stan*, I said grimly to myself. *At age 50 you're virtually a spiritual pauper.*

I knew a little of the Torah but not the spiritual story line or history of our people. Nor did I have even a good overview of what the Bible was all about. So I left the New Testament temporarily to start at the very beginning: Genesis.

In the beginning, I read, God created the heavens and the earth. And God created Adam. Adam was not a Jew. He was a Gentile.

I read on about the sin of Adam and Eve, God's thundering disapproval and the hardships for man that began at this point. The offspring of Adam and Eve seemed pretty worthless until Noah and the cleansing of the flood, I concluded.

Then Abram enters. Abram was a Gentile. But I knew that Abram became Abraham and the father of the Jewish people. How did that happen?

It was the Lord who told Abram, "Get thee out of thy country, and from thy kindred, and from thy father's house, unto a land that I will show thee: and I will make of thee a great nation, and I will bless thee, and make thy name great; and thou shalt be a blessing: and I will bless them that bless thee, and curse him that curseth thee: and in thee shall all families of the earth be blessed."[2]

What a fantastic promise! Even more startling, God said these things when Abram was already 75 years old.

Reading on I found that Abram had obeyed God and left his home and family and went to the land of the Canaanites. And God made good on His promise to Abram:

> Lift up now thine eyes, and look from the place where thou art northward and southward, and eastward and westward: for all the land which thou seest, to thee will I give it, and to thy seed forever.[3]

I felt a surge of elation as I read these verses. God had given this land to my people personally. Meanwhile it had been 24 years since God had first spoken to Abram who was still childless.

> And when Abram was ninety years old and nine, the Lord appeared to Abram, and said unto him, I am the Almighty God; walk before me, and be thou perfect. And I will make my covenant between me and thee. . .[4]

The word "covenant" seemed to leap from the page. What did it mean then between God and man? Between men?

When I looked up the word in reference books, I learned that at the time Abram lived and for centuries before and since, there has been what is called "the cutting of a covenant." This was the highest form of agreement which could be made between two people. It was used on occasions such as when two tribal chiefs wanted to enter into a peace treaty with one another or when they wanted to enter into a mutual defense treaty or when they wanted to demonstrate their love and trust for one another as brothers. A covenant between two people involved total commitment from each to the other.

Invariably "the cutting of a covenant" involved a formal ceremony. The partners would exchange weapons, exchange robes and exchange names. By so doing they were stating that they pledged to one another their strength, their substance and their identity. Then they would recite the blessings for keeping the covenant and the curses which would come if either of them broke the covenant. Next came the actual "cutting." Blood must be shed. Sometimes they would cut faces or arms and then rub their faces or arms together so that the blood would be mingled. Sometimes they would let the blood drip into a bowl, where it was thoroughly mixed to indicate that they were now all one blood. Then each of the partners would drink of the blood.

To "seal" the cutting of the covenant they would rub ashes or some other material into the wound so that it would not heal without leaving a scar. Following the "sealing" of the covenant a "memorial" would be established to remind all who saw it of the covenant. Then the covenant partners would sit together for the "covenant meal." During this feast friends and family members would come and share in their joy as they all formally celebrated the covenant between them.

I turned back to the text in Genesis. When God offered to cut a covenant with Abram, Abram was so overpowered

that he fell to the ground on his face. Abram knew what
cutting a covenant with God meant.

. . . and God talked with him saying,

As for me, behold, my covenant is with thee, and
thou shalt be a father of many nations.

Neither shall thy name any more be called Abram,
but thy name shall be Abraham; for a father of many
nations have I made thee.

And I will make thee exceedingly fruitful . . .[5]

This is my covenant which ye shall keep, between
me and you and thy seed after thee; Every man child
among you shall be circumcised.

And ye shall circumcise the flesh of your foreskin;
and it shall be a token of the covenant betwixt me and
you.[6]

As I read these words, I was stabbed by that word
"token." Yes, I was circumcised, and I knew that circumcision was something that every Jewish male child had to go
through, but I had always thought of circumcision as the
token of our "Jewishness" rather than the token of our
"covenant with God." God had covenanted to be the God
of Abraham's seed. And circumcision was the seal of that
covenant.

Not only did God instruct Abram to circumcise all of his
children but every man-child born in his house. On the day
Abram became Abraham, he and every male in his house
was circumcised.

As I tried to visualize this scene, I shuddered. During
World War II I had been hospitalized for a time. The patient
in the next bed was there to be circumcised. I remembered
what he went through: how painful it had been and how
uncomfortable he was afterwards. I could only guess at the
pain and discomfort all of Abraham's household must have
gone through that day, especially since they were without
all of the medical equipment and painkilling drugs that we
have today.

Obviously, I thought, if these people allowed something so painful to be done to them, they had to have strong motivation. I tried to picture something like that happening today to adult men but couldn't. The people of Abram's day had to have been deeply aware of the importance of this covenant.

To Abram it meant that God was offering Himself as Abram's shield, his defense, his strength. God was giving to Abram His assurance that not only would He prosper Abram safely into old age but that He would make certain that Abram would have sons and heirs and that he would be extremely fruitful. He would be a father of many nations. And God had promised to give to Abram and to his sons all the land of Canaan for an everlasting possession. And then the final promise: not only would God do these things for Abram, but God would be the God of Abram's seed throughout all their generations.

No wonder Abram fell on his face!

To dramatize the seriousness of this covenant—that definitive act which created the Jewish people—God changed Abram's name. He placed an "h," the breath sound of His own name, "Jehovah," into Abram's name. From that day forth he would be known as Abraham.

And I discovered something else. When He changed Abram's name, God modified His own. He would henceforth be known as the God of Abraham to all the world.

Later, God confirmed His covenant with Isaac; still later, with Jacob. Then, 3,500 years later, I was told by my grandparents that the God of Abraham, Isaac and Jacob was my God and the God of my fathers.

But it hadn't penetrated. The words had been, well, just words. And I had never been taught about the covenant.

How was this possible? How was it that I knew Jewish boys had to be circumcised but not why? Why did we never discuss in our home what God meant when He said to

Abraham that He would be God to Abraham's seed?

As I read on through the stories of Isaac, Jacob and Joseph I could see that many of the Jews of that period were not greatly different from today's Jews. There was indifference and ignorance about the basic tenets of our faith. Heroic leaders stood out, but the people faltered. Moses went through this:

> And God spake unto Moses, and said unto him, I am the Lord: and I appeared unto Abraham, unto Isaac, and unto Jacob . . .[7]
>
> And I have also established my covenant with them, to give them the land of Canaan . . .[8]
>
> And I have also heard the groaning of the children of Israel, whom the Egyptians keep in bondage: and I have remembered my covenant.
>
> Wherefore say unto the children of Israel, I am the Lord and I will bring you out from under the burdens of the Egyptians . . .[9]

No sooner had Moses led the children of Israel out of Egypt than the grumblings started. Constantly he had to remind his people of their covenant with God:

> And Moses came and told the people all the words of the Lord and all the judgments: and all the people answered with one voice, and said, all the words which the Lord hath said will we do . . .
>
> And he took the book of the covenant, and read in the audience of the people: and they said, All that the Lord hath said will we do, and be obedient.
>
> And Moses took the blood, and sprinkled it on the people, and said, Behold the blood of the covenant, which the Lord hath made with you concerning all these words.[10]

Reflecting on these verses, I recalled the way in which we observed Passover each year and how our services had almost nothing in them concerning the covenant and what God required of us. We remembered the Exodus, but we said nothing about the covenant. How strange!

Moses recognized that under the terms of the covenant, the Jewish people would no longer be as before. God now directly told them how they were to live. He directed them to be separated from all other people on the earth. They were to be unique. He told them the foods they could and could not eat. He specified the rules under which they were to live. He prohibited them from following the customs of other people. They were to obey Him and Him alone.

The people of Israel received these instructions, promised to obey them and then decade after decade they violated them, committing all manner of sins including intermarriage with Gentiles. God's instructions had been clear yet were disobeyed. How could they undo the wrongs they had done and again come into right standing with God? Ezra, the priest, gave this answer:

> . . . Ye have transgressed, and have taken strange wives, to increase the trespass of Israel. Now therefore make confession unto the Lord, the God of your fathers, and do His pleasure: and separate yourselves from the people of the land and from the strange wives.[11]

I could picture their agony. Thousands of Jewish men had married Gentile women. They had children and had established their family lives. Now they were instructed to leave their wives and children. I shuddered as I put myself in their position.

The people who heard Ezra recognized that he was speaking for the Lord. They knew what covenant meant. They heard God's promised blessings and promised cursings. They felt they had no alternative. They left their wives and children and returned to follow the covenant of God

So it was with God's chosen people. If they were to follow God's commandments, they had to be separate from all other people in the world. Physical contact was forbidden.

Table fellowship was forbidden. Intermarriage was forbidden. The contrast was stark.

1. The Jews had the one and only true God. The Gentiles did not.
2. The Jews had the covenant and God's promises. The Gentiles did not.
3. The Jews had the hope of the Messiah. The Gentiles did not.
4. The Jews were the Chosen of God. The Gentiles were not.

The Gentiles were aliens. They were aliens to the people of God and aliens to the covenant of God. They were helpless. They were hopeless. They were without God.

For the next 1,500 years, the separation between the Jews and the Gentiles became more and more rigid. This separation caused distrust and suspicion, hostility and fear, anger and hatred.

Then Jesus came!

As I sat in my den late one night pondering all I had learned about the covenant, I realized I had not been threatened by my Biblical review of Jewish history. These were facts. But what was I supposed to do with Jesus? What did he have to do with the covenant?

A thought rammed into my mind. If a covenant between two parties usually called for a "cutting" between them, and God had asked His people to be circumcised as their "shedding of blood," then what was the "cutting" on God's side?

The image of Jesus being pierced and bleeding on the cross swam before my eyes. I tried to set it aside. But it wouldn't go away.

I could not run from the issue. I had to get back to my reading of the New Testament and the facing up to the question: Is Jesus the Messiah?

9

The Tension Grows

As I worked harder and harder to build my case for presentation to Judy, it seemed to me that Ethel was becoming much more relaxed about it all. I could hear her and Heidi laughing a lot during their discussions. Although we had agreed not to try to influence each other, one morning as we dressed I challenged Ethel about her casual attitude.

"These jokes you and Heidi share, why not try them on me," I began.

"What jokes?"

"I don't know what jokes. But you and Heidi laugh so much I thought you had some good ones."

Ethel gave me a searching look. "Our laughter bothers you?"

"No, not really. I just wanted to be in on it."

"Let me see . . . " Ethel's brow furrowed as she closed the door of her dresser. "Well, there was one about Judy's children."

"What children? She's not even married."

"Her future children. You don't think that because she's accepted Jesus, she will become a nun or something, do you?"

"I hope not."

"Well, I was saying to Heidi that instead of Judy's children singing 'Had, Gad Ya' at Passover, they'll be singing 'Jesus Wants Me for a Sunbeam'."

"I don't think that's funny, Eth."

"That's what troubles me about you, Stan. The world has not come to an end because Judy believes in Jesus. I know that I was as upset as you in the beginning. Well, I still don't want this for Judy, but the more I read of Jesus, the more I like him."

"That's not the issue," I fumed. "It's not hard to like someone who helps people and is good to children. It's what Jesus says about himself that is at issue."

"Like what?"

"Like I and the Father are one."

"Jesus says he is God."

"That's right."

Ethel was busy tidying up the top of her dressing table. "There's nothing halfway about anything Jesus did," she mused.

"I guess that's what bothers me so much. It's easy to accept him as a good person, a brilliant teacher, even a prophet, but those statements he made about himself drive me up the wall. You have to accept him completely or . . ."

"Or what?"

"Or decide that He was nutty as a fruitcake."

"That's what it boils down to, isn't it? Either it's all true, or it's all false!"

Then Ethel changed the subject.

"Stan, how much longer are you going to go on with this? You can't just forget your business entirely."

"I promise you we won't starve, Eth. This is just something that I have to do no matter how long it takes. Judy has brought us to a crisis of beliefs. I've got to prove that she is wrong."

"What if she is right? Where do we go from there?"

Silence. For me, that was still the final question, and I

didn't want to answer it.

"I'm not sure it's an either-or situation, dear," I said more softly. "Remember, years ago, we said that when our girls grew up we could give them the freedom to make the critical choices in life?"

"Sure I do. But I never thought that it would come to this."

"Nor did I. I'll tell you the truth, Eth. I think I'd be more comfortable if Judy told us that she didn't believe in God than that she believes in Jesus. You can still be a Jew and not believe in God."

"But Stan, why can't she believe in Jesus and still be Jewish?"

"Because being one denies the other."

With that I got up and went back into the den. But the question lingered in my mind, and I knew that my answer was wrong. The early believers were all Jews or proselytes to Judaism. What happened? How did something which started out so Jewish wind up so Gentile? What happened to those early Jewish believers?

At this point I began to read the Book of Acts, and to my surprise answers to the questions I had just asked seemed to fly at me from every page. When Jews who followed Jesus became believers, they continued the life that they had always known. They still followed all of their traditions. Their belief in Jesus did not destroy their identity as Jews.

But there were understandably problems when it came to the way these new Jewish believers related to Gentiles. Peter, in particular, had a difficult time as he thought about Jews mingling with Gentiles. What I read in the 10th chapter of Acts jolted me to my roots.

Peter was in Joppa, praying on the rooftop of the house where he was staying. It was about noon. Peter was hungry and was probably about to head for the dining room when he fell into a trance:

> . . . heaven opened, and something descending,
> like a great sheet, let down by four corners upon the
> earth. In it were all kinds of animals and reptiles and
> birds of the air.
>
> And there came a voice to him, "Rise, Peter; kill and
> eat." But Peter said, "No, Lord; for I have never eaten
> anything that is common or unclean."
>
> And the voice came to him again a second time,
> "What God has cleansed, you must not call common."
> This happened three times, and the thing was taken up
> at once to heaven.[1]

Poor Peter. I could see him on the roof with a stunned
look on his face. How could God direct in the Law that he
was not to eat anything unclean and then tell him in a vision
that he was to eat unclean meat? Unthinkable!

Yet this was God speaking, and to make sure Peter got
the message, it was repeated three times. Then adding to
Peter's inner distress came another directive from God: He
was to go to the house of Cornelius, a Roman centurion,
who lived in Caesarea. Ordinarily Peter would never have
gone inside a Gentile's home. But God's voice and command were unmistakable. Peter left the next day for
Caesarea and was greeted with great deference by Cornelius who asked him to speak to the people he had gathered
inside his home.

Peter began by saying, "Truly I perceive that God shows
no partiality, but in every nation anyone who fears Him
and does what is right is acceptable to Him. Then Peter told
the Gentiles about Jesus—his life and death and resurrection.

> While Peter was still saying this, the Holy Spirit fell on
> all who heard the word. And the believers from among
> the circumcised who came with Peter were amazed, be-
> cause the gift of the Holy Spirit had been poured out
> even on the Gentiles.[2]

The meaning of this chapter couldn't be clearer. Not only did God intend for Jesus to be the Messiah for the Jewish people but for Gentiles as well. Shaking my head, I went on to the 11th chapter of Acts.

When the disciples in Jerusalem heard what had happened in the house of Cornelius, they were most upset. Naturally. But I noticed that their anger was not directed at Peter because he told the Gentiles about Jesus. They were angered because *he went inside the house of Gentiles and ate with them*. They were angry because he had broken the Law establishing the separation between Jews and Gentiles.

God had said in Leviticus 20, "I have severed you from other people, that you should be mine." How could Peter deliberately violate God's law and go in among the Gentiles? On this ground they challenged him.

Peter answered them in the only way he could. He told them of the vision he had received and of what God had done. They reflected upon this miracle, "glorified God" and finally said: "Then to the Gentiles also God has granted repentance unto life."

I felt a bit numb as the impact of that statement sank in. The Bible was saying here that despite 1,500 years of God-directed separation between Jew and Gentile, God was not only offering the Messiah to the Gentiles, he was saying that the Jews and Gentiles were no longer to be divided as they once were.

This was a staggering concept. No wonder the Jewish believers of 35 A.D. had trouble hearing it.

And where I was today, the situation was completely reversed. Then, the Messiah was thought to be only for the Jews. Now, he was thought to be only for the Gentiles. Where could I go from here?

10

What Happened to the Early Believers?

The story of Peter and Cornelius not only jolted my thinking but left me with one big unanswered question. All those early Jewish believers won to Jesus by Paul and the apostles—what had happened to them? To find the answer I had to begin with some history lessons that went back to my high school days.

First, the Roman Empire: how greatly it shaped the history of world religions. When Rome conquered Israel and Judah, the area became one of the most difficult regions for her to govern. Between 7 and 41 A.D. Rome had to send in seven different governors to rule Judea. Their vision of statesmanship was that there was no problem which could not be solved by bloodshed.

When Rome sent Flavius to become the eighth governor, he proved to be even worse than those who came before him. One year during the Passover feast in Jerusalem, Flavius thought it would be great fun to show the Jews his authority and power. He confiscated the robes of the high priest, ridiculed their sacred beliefs, then demanded that the Jews pay 17 talents of gold to him from the Temple treasury. In terms of today's money this was well in excess of $2 million.

That did it. In May 66 A.D. open rebellion broke out in

every Jewish city and village.

Consider how ridiculous was the situation. A few thousand Jews of Palestine were rising in revolt and challenging the greatest military power that the world had ever known. The other conquered nations which comprised the Roman Empire watched in disbelief as little David was preparing to fight the Roman Goliath.

Roman leaders knew that the stakes were high and that the whole world was watching. They knew that if the Jews were to win their independence, there would be no way to keep other nations from rising up, too. Accordingly, Rome set out to destroy the upstarts.

Troops were sent from Rome, battles were fought, but the Jewish fighters were tough and solidly resistant. After the first year of war, Emperor Nero called in his most able general, Vespasian, and gave him full command over the legions he would need. Vespasian moved slowly but thoroughly. The second year moved on, and the third year began. Now it was 68 A.D.

By this time Vespasian had conquered almost all of Judea but he still had not conquered Jerusalem. Time after time his armies went up against the city's wall; time after time they were repulsed.

In 69 A.D. Nero died and the Senate at Rome offered the throne to Vespasian. He accepted it gladly and turned the destruction of Jerusalem over to his son, Titus.

Titus used more than 80,000 troops to surround Jerusalem. He commanded his soldiers to dress in full battle uniform, then staged a military parade around the walls of Jerusalem in an awesome display of Roman might. The parade lasted three days. When it was over, the watching Jews on the ramparts gave the Romans a loud Bronx cheer.

Enraged, Titus attacked. Siege guns hurled rocks at the northern wall of Jerusalem tearing a gaping hole in the fortifications, through which the Roman soldiers poured.

After two weeks of savage, hand-to-hand fighting, the Jews drove the Romans out.

Titus then decided to starve the Jews until they were too weakened for further resistance. To make sure that no food or water supplies would reach the city from the outside, Jerusalem was sealed off from the rest of the world with a high wall of earth. Anyone not a Roman soldier caught anywhere in this vast, dry moat was crucified on the top of the earthen wall in sight of the Jerusalem Jews. As many as 500 people a day were so executed.

The end was inevitable. With battering rams and portable bridges, the Romans again stormed the walls of Jerusalem. A massacre followed. The temple was put to the torch, priests were killed and the zealots were thrown from the walls. Prisoners were earmarked as slaves and taken to Rome. Some were held for the lions in the arena. Others were slaughtered for the amusement of the Roman people.

The account made me proud of the courage of my Jewish forebears, but what I really wanted to know was what was happening to the Jewish believers.

Obviously some were part of the army defending Jerusalem, but very little information was available on this subject. A prophecy in Luke then gave me a hint as to what happened:

> But when ye see Jerusalem compassed with armies, then know that her desolation is at hand. Then let them that are in Judea flee unto the mountains; and let them that are in the midst of her depart out; and let not them that are in the country enter therein. For these are days of vengeance, that all things which are written may be fulfilled. Woe unto them that are with child and to them that give suck in those days! For there shall be great distress upon the land, and wrath unto this people. And they shall fall by the edge of the sword, and shall be led captive into all the nations: and

> Jerusalem shall be trodden down of the Gentiles until
> the times of the Gentiles be fulfilled.[1]

I could imagine the conflict the believers felt as they saw Jerusalem surrounded. They had been instructed to flee and yet had loyalty to family and friends. Obviously many left before the Roman armies completed their task of destroying Jerusalem.

At this point in 70 A.D. the believers were still very much a part of the Jewish community.

I wanted to know more. What had happened then? Where were the history books I needed? I searched my shelves and went to the library. Piece by piece the story of those years came together.

After Jerusalem was destroyed and the Jewish people were dispersed throughout the region, a major crisis developed in Jewish life. Two questions surfaced: How could the Jewish religion function outside the Temple and the sacrificial system? And how could the Jewish people survive if they were forced to live among the Gentile nations? These were critical issues. In time the answers were provided: the synagogue would have to replace the Temple as the center of Jewish life, the rabbi would replace the priest as the spiritual leader, and Biblical Judaism would be replaced by rabbinic Judaism.

To implement the changes, new procedures were created and new rules were promulgated. For Jews who believed in Jesus, these created problems. Many had come to understand and believe that the Messiah, by his death and resurrection, had fulfilled the Mosaic law and that Jews were no longer to be bound by its 613 rules. They argued that since the Temple no longer existed, it was impossible to live by the Law and that Scripture had not established the new rules. Many argued that there was now a new era, an era of grace.

Sincere controversy broke out between the two groups.

There was tension over the fact that many thousands of Jews who believed in Jesus had fled from Jerusalem during the War of 66-70 A.D. and that these believers opposed the new forms of Jewish religious expression. Yet they were still considered to be joined together in the family of Israel.

Over the next decades, however, these tensions within the Jewish community dissolved as a more serious issue emerged—the desire for freedom. It began with taxes. For years each Jew paid a tax to Rome for the support of the Temple in Jerusalem. After the Temple was destroyed, Rome insisted that the Temple tax continue to be paid. It was levied against all Jews, even against non-Jews who were circumcised. The revenues so raised were used to support the temple of Jupiter at Rome. For 26 years this was a terrible affront to the Jewish people until Emperor Nerva repealed the tax in 96 A.D.

Taxes and other pressures from Rome continued to plague the Jewish community. They had to be free. By the year 132 A.D., Rabbi Akiva was able to spearhead the second Jewish revolt against Rome. Akiva had enormous favor with the people, and Jewish men rose to the cause; those who believed in Jesus as well as those who did not were fighting alongside one another and under the banner of freedom.

Then Rabbi Akiva made a terrible mistake. He declared that Simon Ben Kosiba, the general leading the revolt, was Bar Cochba, the "Son of Light," the Messiah. While this rallied most of Jewry, it had an adverse effect upon those who believed that Jesus was the Messiah. They could not fight under the banner of one they believed to be a false messiah. By the thousands they deserted.

The revolt against Rome would have been difficult enough to accomplish if the Jewish army had been at full strength, but with many thousands of men leaving the army, the revolt was doomed to failure. Just as the war in

Jerusalem had lingered on for four horrible years, so this uprising in all of Palestine lasted for more than three. The losses on both sides were heavy. Finally Bar Cochba was put to death, as was Rabbi Akiva and the other leaders of the revolt.

Rome's vengeance against the Jews was swift and stinging. Jerusalem was destroyed and plowed under. It was declared off-limits to all Jews. As the Jewish people suffered under the new tyranny, they did not turn their anger and resentment against Rabbi Akiva for being a false prophet or against Bar Cochba for being a false messiah. They turned their anger against those deserters who considered Jesus as their Messiah.

Anger grew against the believers until the rabbis felt that they had to act. They proclaimed the believers to be traitors. There was to be no contact with them. They were to be ostracized from the Jewish community. They were apostates. Those in desperate need were not to go to the followers of Jesus for help, and certainly no one was to provide help for them.

In the months that followed this pronouncement, the Jewish believers were faced with questions they never anticipated:

1. Should they maintain their belief in Jesus the Messiah even at the cost of leaving the Jewish community?
2. If they did so, could they survive in a Gentile world?
3. Should they reject the Messiah in order to stay within the Jewish community?
4. Could they deny the Messiah publicly, but continue to believe privately?
5. How were they to live?

As the months stretched into years, these questions were answered differently by different believers. Some found that no matter how much they wanted to retain their belief in Jesus, they could not survive outside of the Jewish community. They gave up their beliefs.

Others retained their beliefs but remained silent concerning them. They became secret believers and stayed in the synagogue. Still others entered into the world of the Gentiles and were thoroughly assimilated within it.

One of the early Gentile theologians of the second century, Justin, wrote about the situation facing the Jewish believers. He saw four distinct categories emerging:

1. Those Jews who became part of the Gentile church;
2. Those who remained within the synagogue, as secret believers;
3. Those who became Ebionites;
4. Those who became Nazarenes.

Little is understood among Jews or Gentiles about the latter two groups. Because no canon of Scripture for the new covenant had yet been established, the believers were dependent upon the old covenant, word-of-mouth reports of events which took place, and less-than-complete understanding of the writings of Paul, Peter and James.

The Ebionites (sometimes called the "poor ones") held these beliefs:

1. An insistence on observing a great part of the Jewish law;
2. Refusal to believe the virgin birth;
3. Repudiation of Paul as an apostle;
4. They considered James to be the 12th apostle and called him the "bishop of bishops;"
5. They venerated Peter.

Jesus, claimed the Ebionites, came to fulfill the law and the prophets as a new Moses. He took from the law all of the false doctrines which were added after Moses died—as, for example, the sacrificial system—and he emphasized the essence of the true law: the laws of purification and of the virtues of poverty and vegetarianism and asceticism.

Theologian F. F. Bruce notes that the Ebionites "thought

of themselves as forming a bridge between catholic Christianity and Jewish orthodoxy, combining and conserving all that was of value in both, while rejecting the errors of both. If they hoped to reconcile these two on an Ebionite basis, they were disappointed. The orthodox Jews disowned them as apostates; the orthodox Christians disowned them as heretics."

It is believed that the Ebionites lived on until the seventh century, but little more is known about them.

In contrast to the Ebionites, the Nazarenes held that:

1. Jesus was the Messiah;
2. He was the Son of God;
3. His teachings were superior to Moses and the prophets;
4. Christians of Jewish descent should observe the Jewish practices of circumcision, sabbath observance and dietary laws.

While the Nazarenes kept many of the Jewish customs, they did not insist that it was compulsory for non-Jews to keep them.

As the controversies continued within the Jewish community, Christianity was now established and growing throughout the Gentile world. Hundreds of thousands of Gentiles became believers. Before long there were many times more Gentile believers than Jewish believers. As a result, new controversies arose. Without a background in Jewish history or Jewish life, it became difficult for Gentiles to understand why the Jewish believers wanted to continue to do the things they had always done before accepting Jesus as Messiah.

One of the major controversies concerned resurrection day. The Jewish believers insisted that it must be held on the third day of Passover: the 17th day of Nisan (which covers the latter part of March and early April). But since Passover was celebrated according to the Jewish calendar and not in accordance with the calendar used by the rest of the world, the 17th of Nisan was not a meaningful date to the Gentiles. They wanted to fix a date which had meaning on their calendars. In 196 A.D., at a council meeting in Cesarea, it was determined that resurrection day would be celebrated on a Sunday each year during the Feast of Eshtar. That decision produced Easter Sunday.

The Jewish believers were not represented on the council making this decision. When they learned what had been done, they were crushed. "God gave us the date for Passover, and Jesus rose on the third day of Passover! How can you change this date?" they cried.

But the Gentiles were not listening. After removing resurrection day from the Passover holiday, it was easy for the Gentiles to take the next step: reject the Passover entirely. This they then did. Passover had no meaning for them.

And so the gulf widened.

By 325 A.D. official proclamations were being made within the Gentile Christian church that resurrection day was to be observed on Easter Sunday by *all* believers. A few years later, another council meeting was held in Antioch. It announced that anyone attempting to celebrate the Passover on the 17th day of Nisan was to be excommunicated.

Obviously the Gentiles were determined to confront all Jewish believers: "We are now the majority. Come all the way with us or go back to Judaism. There is no middle ground."

As the centuries rolled forward, the church pulled further and further back from its Jewish roots. Soon it would even deny that it had such roots. The Jewish people as a whole would be charged with deicide in connection with Christ's death. The degeneration gained momentum through the Crusades and the Inquisition to the pogroms. Then came the "final solution to the Jewish question:" six million Jews murdered in the concentration camps of Nazi

Germany, a self-labeled "Christian" nation.

How could the Jewish people identify with those who killed their people? Impossible!

How could the message of love be so distorted over the centuries into this message of hate?

My search had come a long way. The pieces in the puzzle were fitting together. My understanding of my people's history had greatly increased. But where was I now in connection with question four? Did I believe that Jesus was the Messiah?

Firmly, I shook my head. No way!

11

Point of Crisis

I completed this review of church history late one evening in my den. Although aware that it was a superficial coverage, one overwhelming conclusion stayed with me for weeks. No wonder most Jews today have such a violent reaction when they learn of a Jew who accepts Jesus. History showed that Jews who accepted Jesus as Messiah were not welcomed by most Christians. They were expected to "convert," to stop being Jews. Because of the long heritage of hatred, fear and hostility, division continued to run deep.

At this moment I felt I had a handle on the answer I wanted to give to Judy: "Stay away from Christians. They don't want you really. Let me show you proof of this from history."

Then I sat back in my chair and pondered. Jesus was a Jew. He chose Jews as disciples. During his life on earth nearly all his friends and followers were Jews. He stated that his mission was to the "lost sheep of the house of Israel." Not until Pentecost did the outreach toward other races and nationalities begin on God's instigation. But God could have hardly intended for a work begun by a Jew amid Jews to become an exclusively non-Jewish, world religion.

Man had obviously brought this about, not God.

I stirred uneasily. My grip on the handle was slipping away. Why couldn't I just stop now and present my case to Judy?

Deep down, I sensed it wasn't a strong enough case. It was built on a negative approach. *Don't do it, Judy, because Christians will hurt you. Haven't they always?*

My case gave no positive direction for Judy to go. From her viewpoint it would only be a retreat backward into an unsatisfactory area of confusion and uncertainty.

Angrily I stood up and walked over to the window, looking moodily out at the darkened houses across the street. What was wrong with me? Three months ago I wouldn't have hesitated to use the facts garnered in my search as a weapon. I would have thrown them at Judy with all my energy. Why not now?

Something had changed inside me during those three months. What was it? I had uncovered no scientific logic that convinced me I should accept Jesus as Messiah. If anything, logic dictated a flight from all this digging and questioning before I lost everything I had worked more than twenty years to achieve.

Then what was wrong with me?

At this point in my search, I felt a need to return to my business. (Or was I reluctant to push ahead any further on my self-examination?) I had been invited to address the 1975 convention of the "Million Dollar Round Table" in San Francisco in mid-June. It was a big honor and one which I would not refuse.

As I packed for the trip, I made sure to include my Bible and some of the other study materials I felt I would need. Ethel did not accompany me because wives of the Round Table members are not invited to the convention.

The flight from Washington, D.C., to San Francisco can be a bore, but it was no bore for me. I finished the Book of Revelation in the air as we flew over Denver. I remember the glances of other passengers as I propped the Bible open before me, smoking freely and sipping Jack Daniels while I read.

Perhaps I was overly self-conscious, but I was certain that several of them recognized that I was Jewish. *What's a Jew doing reading the New Testament?* was the question I read in several faces. I tried to ignore these thoughts but they persisted.

As we began our descent into San Francisco, my thoughts turned to Ann. Just a few weeks before she had graduated from Walt Whitman High School and had been accepted for fall admission to the Maryland Institute/College of Art.

For a graduation present Ann wanted us to permit her to visit Neal, one of her best Jewish friends and a fellow artist who lived in Los Angeles. They had practically grown up together during the previous four years. Much as I liked Neal, there was no way that I was going to permit Ann to visit him alone.

A telephone call had then come from Neal. He fully understood how I felt and understood my reluctance to let Ann go. But, he stressed, he had the highest regard for Ann and for us, and there was no way he would permit anything to happen to her while she was with him. Furthermore, he would arrange for Ann to stay with a young woman he knew.

Ethel and I talked about it at length. Ann was almost 18 and a high school graduate. In a few months she would be off to college and away from our control. Did we trust her or didn't we? We had to let her go.

So Ann had left for Los Angeles the day before.

My thoughts then turned to Ethel. Where was she in her spiritual quest? We had not talked about it lately, reluctant to interfere with each other's inner struggle. Ethel had such a strong identity with Judaism. Nothing could ever change that. She would be visiting Judy in Boston while I was gone, and I would call her there.

The excitement of San Francisco consumed me for several days. I enjoyed meeting with old friends from all over the country who were also attending the convention. Our panel worked hard and was well received by the thousands of Round Table members in attendance. My remarks brought me much favorable attention. It was heady stuff.

I tried to get involved with all the partying too, but to my surprise I had no taste for it. One or two drinks was my limit. I couldn't identify with the gossip and found myself recoiling from the endless dirty stories. What was wrong with me? It just wasn't the same as before. My mind was on something else.

I was sharing a room with an old friend and business associate from Washington who was not Jewish. On an impulse I told him about Judy and what I had been going through. His mouth dropped open, and I thought his eyes would bulge right out of his head as I talked. He couldn't understand it; he couldn't relate to it. I wished I had kept my mouth shut.

When I called Ethel from San Francisco, she sounded awful, said she was dizzy and turned the phone over to Judy.

"I think she may be coming down with the flu," Judy explained. "But don't worry, I'm watching her. If she gets worse, I'll call a doctor."

When the convention ended, I flew to Los Angeles to spend a day with my niece, Emilie, a dance teacher in Studio City. Since Ann and Neal were also in Los Angeles, we all met briefly before I caught my plane to Washington. Ann looked surprisingly radiant; I wanted to talk to her, but there was no way for us to be alone or to talk seriously in front of Emilie or Neal.

When I arrived at National Airport in Washington, Ethel was waiting for me. She had returned from Boston the night before and said she was now feeling fine.

As we drove home I was in a glow about the recognition I had received at the Round Table convention and gave her the full picture, omitting only the conversation with my roommate. "How was your time with Judy?" I finally asked.

"We had a wonderful visit."

When I looked startled, she quickly added. "I didn't argue with her, dear. We just visited mostly. She's as convinced as ever that Jesus is the Messiah."

There was silence for several moments. "Stan, where are you now in the search? I mean, have you given it up? Are you going back to work?"

"No, I haven't given it up. There is some work I must do at the office, but then I plan to get back to my reading."

I wasn't sure, but I sensed a slight look of relief on my wife's face. I tried to probe this. "Do you think I should go back to the business?"

She didn't answer right away. "I think you should do what you feel you must do."

That Friday night, Ethel and I again went to services at Beth Messiah where we had made a number of friends. I was startled to learn that there was to be a National Convocation of Messianic Jews two weeks later at a place called Messiah College in Grantham, Pennsylvania. The news that there were enough Messianic Jews to have a national convention, almost blew my mind. How many Messianic Jews could there be?

While I had no intention of going to the convention, I suddenly found myself looking at the program and asking questions about the speakers and about how one gets to

Grantham, Pennsylvania.

When we got home, I asked Ethel if she would like to go to the convention. She thought a while and said that she didn't feel up to it. "But I really do think you should go, Stan," she said firmly.

I considered it off and on for the next few days and then decided that I should go. I needed to do some additional research. A few days later I deposited my bag and briefcase in the trunk of my BMW and took off for Messiah College. The date was July 1, 1975.

My travel directions were specific, and I had no trouble finding Grantham. As I drove into the entrance to the college there before my eyes was a large banner containing the Star of David and the words: "Welcome to Messiah '75."

I parked the BMW and headed for the registration booth. As I walked, I noticed that most of the other people heading for the entrance were Jewish. Yet there were Gentiles in the group as well. All greeted one another and me warmly with big smiles. The atmosphere was sharply in contrast to the cold, professionalism of the convention I had just come from in San Francisco.

After registration, I headed for the big gym where the meetings were held. As I walked inside I was struck by the Jewish music being played and by the fact that there were 700 to 800 people there.

I am an experienced convention-goer, having attended at least 40 conventions during the past 20 years. In the process I have learned how to "work" a convention. You begin with a goal: get the most out of every meeting and every conversation. You look over the program carefully, decide which speakers you need to hear and then spot the people at the meetings you believe can help you. From then on it is work, work and more work. I would meet with anyone whom I thought could help me, always probing for more information. This convention was going to be no different.

After the morning meetings ended, I headed for the
dorm area. On the way out of the building, I saw a woman
who was obviously disabled. She was having great difficul-
ty carrying her suitcase as she walked, and I offered to help
her. As we walked, we became acquainted. Her name was
Lillian. She was Jewish and from Philadelphia. She was
about 60 years of age, and I knew that from the lines in her
face, she had had a very hard life. But you couldn't tell this
from her attitude. She was pleasant and confident and enthusiastic.

As we walked along, she said, "Tell me, Stan, for how
long have you been a believer?"

"I'm not a believer," I quickly replied. "An inquirer,
perhaps, but absolutely not a believer."

"I see."

When we came to a concrete bench, Lillian stopped.
"Let's sit down and rest a moment," she said. Then after
we were seated, she turned to me. "Do me a favor. Open
my briefcase and take out my Bible."

I did so.

"Please open the Bible to Exodus the 20th chapter and
read the first few verses for me," she asked.

I read: "I am the Lord thy God which have brought thee
out of the land of Egypt, out of the house of bondage. Thou
shalt have no other gods before me."

"Enough, Stan. Please close the Bible. Tell me, who is
your god?"

I looked at Lillian as if she had just hit me in the face.
What a question!

"Don't be upset," she said, "I'm not trying to aggravate
you. Just think about it. Who is your god? Whom do you
worship? What do you worship? Do you worship money?
Your family? Your home? Your job? What is it you worship?
Do you worship the God of Abraham, Isaac and Jacob who
delivered our ancestors from the land of Egypt?"

The silence between us grew uncomfortable, but Lillian sat there calmly, in no hurry to move on. It was a hot day. I was perspiring, partly from the walk, partly from the question. Why did it seem so sharply pointed?

Why couldn't I give her a smooth answer? *I believe in the God of Abraham, Isaac and Jacob. But you know how it is, Lillian. Like most people, too often I worship the false gods.*

But the smooth answer remained stuck in my throat. Stuck there because with sudden luminosity another thought intruded. A thought so big and startling that it temporarily paralyzed my tongue.

12

Decision

Lillian had touched something deep inside me that morning. My thoughts were exploding. For the rest of the day I had trouble focusing on the other speakers because of the pressure building up within me. I needed to think.

By the next day—July 2, 1975—little had changed. I had thought so hard my mind seemed scrambled. It was very hot.

I was sharing a room in the dorm with one of the men who had come up from Beth Messiah for the conference. The room wasn't air conditioned. It felt like 95 degrees outside and more than a hundred inside. Sleep wouldn't come. I tossed and turned. I was in agony.

Shortly before midnight, I remember whispering, "Art, are you awake?" Art had been having trouble sleeping, too. We talked for a moment or so and then I said, "Art, would you please do me a favor and pray for me?" As far as I knew that was the first time I had ever asked anyone to pray for me.

Art offered up a very simple prayer that God would give me peace and resolve my deep inner conflict.

I thanked Art and the next thing I knew it was 7 A.M., and I was wide awake. I slipped out of the room quietly so as not to awaken Art and headed towards the dining room for breakfast. There I sat down with the same people with whom I had been having most of my meals. Normally one of them would pray over the food while I remained silent, head bowed. But this morning was different.

"Stan, would you lead us in prayer?"

Startled, I looked up. The dining room was beginning to fill with people and the noise level was rising. I was not a praying man, but I opened my mouth. "Praised be Thou, O Lord our God, King of the universe. I thank You for the fellowship and friendship at this table. I thank You for what we have learned at this meeting. I ask You now to bless this food, and I do so in the name of Jesus, the Messiah."

For a moment I sat there amazed. I had prayed in the name of Jesus, the Messiah! It had not been planned by me. But the words had come from my heart.

The others at the table could have missed it, but they didn't. They all knew of my inner struggles. Their faces were suddenly jubilant.

"Stan, you're a believer! Praise God!" They got up in turn and hugged me. Several cried with joy.

And then I too began to cry.

The decision had been made within me while I was sitting on the stone bench struggling to answer Lillian's questions. In a few moments it seemed that my whole life had passed before me. Who is my God? Everything else had been more important to me than God.

Struggling to answer Lillian, I had said to myself: *Without any doubt I believe in the God of my fathers, the God of Abraham, Isaac and Jacob. I believe that the Bible is God's inspired Word. And I believe that Jesus is the Messiah."*

You believe what, Stan?

The question had been hurled silently by myself, to myself, there on the stone bench. Part of me pulled back, aghast. Part of me bulled on ahead, repeating, *I believe that Jesus is the Messiah*.

A war was going on inside me, Lillian, that hot summer day back in 1975 after you asked me those questions. Ever since, I've wondered how you happened to choose the place, the time and the questions. The answer is, of course, that you didn't.

After the hugs and smiles around the breakfast table and after my own tears had stopped, I was able to recognize that despite the weeks of counting the cost, the overwhelming truth was greater than the cost. The power of truth was greater than the power of fear. An enormous load had been lifted from my heart. Inside of me a singing began to come forth, a joy I had never experienced before, and I reveled in it.

It was late morning when I thought again of Ethel. I must tell her of my decision. Sudden guilt ripped through me. I rushed for the phone.

Then I paused with trepidation and began to plan a scenario of exactly how I would tell her what had happened. The more I tried to plan it, the worse I felt. How would Ethel take it? Would she feel betrayed by me as she had with Judy? And Ann? Would her anger now be directed at me? Would this split our family in two? Cold dread was sweeping over me.

When Ethel answered the phone, I couldn't remember the scenario. All I could do was blurt out: "Eth! It's me! It's over! I've made my decision! Jesus is the Messiah!"

There was a momentary pause as I held my breath. Then Ethel's voice came back softly: "Thank God! That makes it unanimous! We've been waiting for you."

13

Family United

When I hung up the phone after talking to Ethel, I was awestruck. Both Ethel and Ann were believers too. They weren't when I left for San Francisco. What had happened?

Bewildered but happy, I said warm goodbyes to loving new friends made at Messiah College and turned the BMW for home.

When she greeted me, Ethel was amused at my amazement. "You were too preoccupied, Stan, to notice the change in me." Then Ethel described the series of events which had convinced her.

First had come angry, stony resistance. During March, April and May there had been numerous sessions with Heidi. Always low-keyed, empathetic, loving and patient, Heidi was an effective disciple. She never lost her composure in the face of our frustration, disbelief and resentment.

The change, imperceptible at first, began when Ethel started reading the Bible. Like me, she was looking for a weapon to tear down what Judy believed, and she continued to read the Bible as she searched.

Ethel had trouble pinpointing the exact moment of decision. "It happened several days before I went to Boston—while you were getting ready to leave for San Francisco. I had gone to bed the night before, still believing that

101

while Jesus was a good man, He was not who He said He was. When I awoke in the morning I knew it was true. *Jesus was the Messiah*. Do you understand how it could happen this way, Stan?"

I nodded and told her how my heart was suddenly changed, too, while sitting on the stone bench on the Messiah College campus. I had used almost superhuman energy to study different Bibles and many books over a period of some 90 days. I had talked to a wide assortment of knowledgeable people. All the words and opinions and ideas I had jammed into my head had left me totally confused. Then in a quiet way God had touched me, and suddenly it all came together, making perfect sense.

Ethel nodded excitedly as she listened to my story. "Neither one of us made a conscious decision. It was made for us in our hearts."

"Did you call Judy and tell her?" I asked.

Ethel shook her head. "The day I was supposed to leave for Boston, I was sick with chills, fever and nausea. I was confused over what had happened to me spiritually. I didn't know whether I should go to bed or to Boston. But something inside me seemed to say Boston."

"You sure sounded bad when I called from San Francisco."

When I got to Judy's apartment," Ethel continued, "I felt so terrible I went right to bed. Judy wanted to call a doctor. I told her no, that I'd be all right after a good night's sleep."

"And you still hadn't told Judy that you were a believer?"

"No. I really wasn't sure what had happened to me, what with the chills and fever. The next day I felt terrible, but I pretended to feel better so Judy wouldn't worry about me. She saw through me though."

"How could you tell?"

"She asked me if her friend, Charles, could come over and pray for me. I didn't want to see anybody, but Judy was so anxious to do this that I couldn't say no."

"Was this Charles the brother of the young man who had tried to commit suicide?"

"Yes. He was the man who became a believer while in prison and who took Judy to her first church service. He came to Judy's apartment that evening. First, he sat down and told me his story. Twelve years in jail he spent. Imagine! I looked at him and could not believe he had ever done anything bad. He was so kind and gentle, so full of love."

Ethel's eyes filled with tears at the memory. "Then he asked if he could pray for my complete recovery. I was embarrassed, but feeling so sick I said yes. As he prayed and asked God to heal me, I found myself asking God to heal me, too, but for a different reason. I wanted God to heal me for Charles' sake. He was so sincere and so sweet. When he finished praying, Charles was certain that I had been healed. He told me to call him when I felt better, no matter what the time."

I held Ethel's hand as she continued the story. "As soon as Charles left I felt very nauseous and headed for the bathroom. After a few moments, Judy knocked on the door and came in to be with me. I was sitting on the bathroom floor holding my head. We talked for about five minutes when, suddenly, I realized that I was feeling better. I didn't know when the change came over me, but I was feeling much better. I got up, very excited, turned to Judy and said, 'I haven't eaten for almost three days, and I'm starved. What have you got to eat in this house?'

"We both laughed and headed for the kitchen. Outside of regular meal-type food, all Judy had in the refrigerator was some fresh liverwurst, rye bread and mustard. Not a very good selection for one who had been sick to her stomach and running a fever. I said, 'Well, if God has really healed me, then I can eat anything and it won't hurt me.

Right?' We laughed again, and I fixed myself a real hero sandwich. It tasted great and there were no after effects. I was well."

It was at this point that Ethel told Judy how she had awakened three days before with the sudden awareness that she believed in Jesus. Judy was overwhelmed, and they shed tears together. It was Judy who pointed out to her mother how important the trip to Boston was in the confirmation of her new belief. "God is doing a work in all our hearts," Judy said, much more a prophetess than she realized.

Ann's story was equally amazing. Very hostile to Judy's decision at first, she gradually softened her attitude towards her sister, helped no doubt by the way Ethel had adjusted to it. Her heartbreak had been that Judy had deserted her. As the months went by, the pain lessened but was still very real.

Then came her graduation from high school and the trip to Los Angeles to see Neal. Right away she knew there was something different about her old friend. It didn't take Neal long to tell Ann what it was. He was a believer. He too had accepted Jesus as his Messiah.

I won't even try to tell Ann's story. She will do that one day in her own way, but here is an approximation of the telephone conversation that Ann had with her sister several days later:

"Hi Jude! It's Ann. Guess what?"

"Oh, Ann, I so wanted you to call. What's happened?"

"You won't believe this, Jude. I hardly believe it myself."

"Believe what?"

"I've been visiting Neal for the past few days. Neal has become a believer like you!"

"Ann, that's wonderful. I'm so glad for him."

"That isn't all, Jude."

"Go on."

"It happened to me, too. Last night."

"Ann, don't kid me."

"It's true, Judy. I've accepted Jesus as my Messiah and Lord. I can't wait to see you and tell you everything."

"Ann, I'm crying for joy. Have you told Mom and Dad yet?"

"No, I'm almost afraid to. This could really split our family."

"No, it won't Ann. We all love each other. Tell the truth, and God will work it out so that our whole family will be closer than ever."

"You'll help me if I get stuck?"

"I sure will. Oh, Ann, it's just like old times. I'm so happy."

"Me too, Jude. I love you."

14

The Final Question

There was still one unanswered question at the end of my list of five. If I believe that Jesus is the Messiah, what does that do to me?

Accepting Jesus as my Messiah and Lord was an earth-shaking decision for me. But after I made it, I was exhilarated and wanted to learn as much about Him as I could learn. I wanted to be with other believers and talk about the Lord and about the Bible. I wanted to share the thrill they talked about of "flowing in the Spirit." I wanted to learn more about what it meant to be a new creation and what this would do to the rest of my life. I felt that I had to make up for all of those lost years.

Before long I was going to nine meetings a week in addition to running my business. This went on for many months, and I loved every minute of it. But it was wearing. Both Ethel and I had to learn to be more selective. The human body can stand only so much. When things settled down, we had reduced our activity to four meetings each week.

Soon after I became a believer, one of my friends told me that based upon his experience I ought to maintain a low profile for months, possibly years, before trying to tell the outside world what had happened to me. I thought that this was good advice. Not that I would deny anything if asked, but I felt I should really know what I was talking about before I got up on any platform.

But Ethel hadn't received that advice. When a friend invited her to come on her radio program as a guest and share what God was doing in her life, Ethel quickly agreed.

Ethel and I did discuss it, and I was a bit apprehensive, but since the show was to be aired on a Saturday morning over a local Christian radio station, I felt it would be all right to do it. Certainly none of our old friends would be tuned to that kind of a station.

Not so. A secretary in my sister's office heard the broadcast, was overjoyed by the story and recognized Ethel's name. She carried the news to my sister, Dorris, who was not delighted. As a result of what she was told, our relationship all but terminated.

One day weeks later, Dorris said, "Look Stan, you're my brother and that's that. But please—I don't want to hear one word about what you think or what you believe. Do you understand me?"

I understood her all right. The news about our family soon spread throughout the community. Immediately, we began to be aware of heads turning from us when we entered the supermarket and met neighbors. Invitations stopped coming. Cold stares and tightened lips greeted us on the social scene. We had told no one about anything, but the rumor mill had already accused, tried and convicted us. The sentence? Isolation.

Now this wasn't true of all our friends. Some picked up the phone and called to ask, "What's happened to you?" Others came over and wanted to know the truth. Those who were truly our friends behaved beautifully. Since we had never discussed God with them before, had never discussed what we did or did not believe about the Scriptures or Bible prophecy or the Messiah or anything else having to do with these issues, they determined that our relationship was not based upon them, and they remained constant.

But there were trying moments for every member of our family.

A few months after word got out that we had become "Messianic Jews" (which after analysis was interpreted "Christian" by most Jews), I attended an all-day seminar sponsored by our local trade association. Between speeches I encountered a man I had known for more than 20 years. We had been students together, had worked within the association on many committees, were both involved in the United Jewish Appeal. When I stopped to chat with him for a moment, my greeting was met with stony silence and an icy look.

Surprised, I said to him: "Hey, Frank, what's the matter? What have I done to deserve a greeting like that?"

At first he refused to respond. When I persisted, he glared at me. "Look, Stan, I've got nothing to say to you. I wish I didn't know you. As far as I am concerned you're nothing but a rotten traitor! You've become a lousy Jesus freak. I've got to protect my people from people like you."

With that he turned away, but sorely wounded I snapped back, "What do you mean by a crack like that? How do you know anything about me and what I believe? How dare you say that you have to 'defend your people from people like me'!"

Frank's retort: "Look you SOB, if I have to spell it out for you, you're dumber than I thought."

And with that, he turned on his heel and walked away. I was crushed and angry. But I took it. I thank God for the grace He poured out on me at that moment.

A few nights later, Ann came home in tears. She had been at a party with a number of her old high school friends. While some of them were Gentiles, most were Jewish. During the course of the evening, one of the Gentile boys asked her, "Hey Ann, is it true that you and your whole family have become Jesus freaks?"

Ann was stunned by the question, especially since it was asked in front of all of her other friends. She didn't know how to answer other than to tell the truth. As she did so, the "friend" turned on her. "Don't you tell me about Jesus. What do you know about Him anyway?" And with that he began to taunt and embarrass her, forcing her to flee in tears. She was crushed.

Ethel had her bad moments too. Shortly after we became believers, she was shopping in one of the local discount stores. One of our former neighbors came up to her and, in a harsh and angry voice, asked: "Is what I hear about you true?"

Ethel was a bit flustered by the intensity of the question. "I don't know. What have you heard about me?"

"That you and your whole family have become Jews for Jesus."

"Well," said Ethel, "that's an organization out on the west coast. We don't belong to it, but we are Jews who believe that Jesus is the Messiah. If you want to know why, I'll be happy to talk with you about it some time."

"No thank you," came the reply. Then she spit in Ethel's face.

As Ethel described the incident, she said, "I was shocked. Spitting in my face was bad enough, but as I considered her background and the possible reasons for her doing this, it made no sense. Neither she nor any member of her family belongs to a synagogue, nor do they have any religious beliefs as far as I know. When her son was 13 and should have been ready for his Bar Mitzvah, she threw a big party for him, and he gave a cello recital instead. How can she ignore God, the Bible and all Jewish practices as if they didn't exist and then attack me for my beliefs?"

Once again, the secular history of the past 2,000 years

had so inflamed emotions that the real issue was hidden in the smoke. Then the familiar pattern emerged again: fear, withdrawal, anger and rejection.

It didn't take long for the effect to be felt on my business. One accountant whom I had known for years and who had been referring business to me because he appreciated the thoroughness of my service, suddenly called to tell me that we would no longer be working together. He explained that he felt very badly about it but that his wife was so incensed over the fact that I believed in Jesus that she absolutely insisted that he stop working with me. I had never met his wife.

While none of my clients called to cancel their insurance with me because of my new beliefs, I knew that there was a pulling back in some quarters. More withdrawal. More attempts at isolation.

But not everyone behaved in this manner.

Mabel, a woman we had known for more than 30 years, was one of Ethel's closest friends. She stood like a rock against all who attacked us. She refused to concede that either Ethel or I had stopped being Jewish. She was angry and hurt for us. Many times she came to Ethel in love and said, "I just don't understand it. You and Stan have one of the best marriages of any of our friends. You have a great relationship with your kids. Stan makes an excellent living. You have a magnificent home. You've got everything that most people would give their eye teeth for. Why do you need to be involved with this Jesus?"

As we shared with Mabel the inner joy of our experience, we could feel the pain Mabel felt for us, and we loved her very much for it.

But I had the answer to my question about what believing in Jesus does to a Jewish family. It tests us and our new beliefs. We suddenly learn about a new kind of persecution.

Throughout this entire period, God sustained us with His grace and His love. We refused to allow anything to rob us of our joy or our victory while we adjusted to the tumultuous changes in our lives.

15

How Shall I Now Live?

For nine months after my experience at Messiah College, I had an excitement in my life that wouldn't quit. Nor had I ever felt anything like it before. It was a bubbling joy, a lightness, a freedom, an awareness of the presence of God that I could not explain to anyone who had not experienced it.

I'm sure most new believers experience this same euphoria. Answers to prayer seem almost automatic. Vexing personal problems are somehow easier to handle. My chain smoking, for example. After smoking for more than 30 years I had tried numerous times to quit, using hypnosis, will power, psychology. Nothing worked.

It came to a head soon after my big decision when I began attending a men's prayer breakfast on Tuesday mornings. I was the only smoker. It was embarrassing. Finally, I got down to cases with the Lord, admitted I couldn't stop on my own power, then asked Him to take away my desire for tobacco. He did! I have never smoked since.

That very instant the desire to smoke left me. I kept a pack in my pocket for weeks, then threw it away.

There was an ease and fluidity to nearly every aspect of our lives for almost nine months. Then suddenly the "high" ended. I was very upset. What had I done wrong? I discussed this with some of my friends who were older than me in the Lord. They laughed and told me it was God's way of telling me that I had to grow up. It was time to get off the emotional highs and lows of feelings and begin to discover what faith is. It was time for me to discover what God had for me to do.

This last thought was almost too much. I was stunned at the prospect that God had a specific something that He wanted *me* to do. What could I possibly do for God?

As a Jewish believer, I knew that I had become an oddity. While I was still perfectly comfortable with my identity as a Jew, most Jews did not feel comfortable with me. Old wounds and old conditioning rose to the surface in many of them, and the Jewish community as a whole looked at our family in disbelief.

The Jewish community is able to understand and accept the fact that there are Orthodox Jews, Conservative Jews, Reconstructionist Jews, Humanistic Jews, Agnostic Jews, Atheistic Jews—even Gay Jews. No matter how they all feel about God, they are still Jews. But somehow Messianic Jews, those Jews who believe in God and also believe that Jesus is the Messiah, are different. For them the welcome mat is often pulled away.

But Gentiles can also be a problem. Some believing and nonbelieving Gentiles have bought the big lie that a Jew cannot believe in Jesus and still be a Jew. Thus they tend to look at us as if we are freaks.

With some Gentile believers too much attention creates a problem for us. They are so thrilled to see Bible prophecy being fulfilled before their eyes, seeing Israel as a nation again, seeing Jews coming to Jesus as Messiah in numbers not seen for 2,000 years, that we are in danger of becoming "pets" or "mascots." Often our new brothers and sisters are more interested in the fact that we are "Jewish" believers than that we are just new "believers."

In the months that followed I faced still another dilemma. It involved almost all of the Messianic Jews I had come to know. Most of them were brought up in nominally Jewish homes where the reality of God and the Bible were missing from their lives. Once they became believers they developed a tremendous hunger for roots. They wanted to know more and more about their identity as Jews and about things Jewish. When pressure or rejection came at them they felt threatened and turned instinctively to one another for fellowship and support.

The pattern was almost universal and it led to the question, "How are we to live now that we believe?"

Like a wild cancer cell, the controversy spread. I learned that it had been going on for years. In some ways the clock had been turned back 1,800 years as the old questions rose again: How are we Jews to function in what is primarily a Gentile world? Do we remain separate from Gentile believers, or do we worship with them? If we are to worship with them, will we have to go into churches? Won't this lead to assimilation? Mustn't this be avoided at all costs? Should we strive to create a synagogue for our worship? If so which kind, Orthodox, Conservative or Reform? If we establish synagogues what will happen to our Gentile brothers and sisters who want to worship with us? Won't this make them feel like second class citizens? If that happens, won't we be violating the Bible which tells us that we are to be "one in the Body?" Is our concentration on preserving things Jewish, fear of man or a type of idolatry? How are we to reconcile the Word of God with the cultural differences and fears that still exist? How are we to preserve our identity as Jews?

Round and round the discussions continued.

I joined other Jewish believers as we wrestled with these questions. There were very articulate and emotional arguments raised in many quarters. The problem was not local. It was national. Strangely, only in Israel was this problem not a problem. There the Jewish believers were not threatened by loss of identity as Jews. They knew that they were Jews, and no one could take that from them.

Several groups had already decided that the answer lay in becoming *more* Jewish than ever. This was the extreme right. Others who abandoned almost all Jewish customs swung to the extreme left. The controversy raged at meetings. Over coffee. At conferences. Via long distance telephone calls which ran long into the night. We talked and talked and talked.

Throughout all this time, I searched the Scriptures. There I found what for me appeared to be God's direction. Jesus had said:

> Blessed are you, when men shall revile you and persecute you, and shall say all manner of evil against you falsely, for my sake.[1]
> And ye shall be hated of all men for my name's sake: but he that endureth to the end shall be saved.[2]
> There is no man that hath left house, or parents, or brethern, or wife, or children, for the Kingdom of God, who shall not receive manifold more in this present time, and in the world to come everlasting life.[3]

The message was pointed: we believers were to expect persecution from the world. And even from our own family. But those willing to endure hardship will in time receive manifold blessings.

Peter had similar words of advice. When he wrote his first letter to the Jewish believers they were fearing for their very lives. The oppressor then was Rome. Nero proclaimed that these believers were responsible for the great fire which destroyed much of the city. They were hunted down mercilessly. When caught, they would be covered with pitch and set on fire to provide light in Nero's gardens or would be brought into the arena to provide food for the lions or sport for the gladiators.

When Peter wrote to his fellow Jews, he did not look at
their circumstances nor did he look backward. He looked
forward. He told them of their inheritance, their reward.
God, Himself, was safeguarding it for them, and it was in-
corruptible and unfading. Peter knew the pressures the believers were under, but he did not focus attention on the
pressures. He put the focus upon the Word of God. He told
them to feast on the Word of God, to call out for the un-
adulterated spiritual milk.

Then he told them what was really at stake. He said that
they had come to the Living Stone, despised indeed by men
but chosen and greatly honored by God. They had a responsibility even in the face of the pressures they faced;
they were to be built up into a spiritual house of God; they
were a holy priesthood, able to offer spiritual sacrifices
which were acceptable to God by Jesus the Messiah.

Peter's advice was very specific:

> . . . be calm, self-controlled, men of prayer. Above
> everything else be sure that you have real deep love for
> each other, remembering how love can cover a multi-
> tude of sins.[4]

> Be men of good and holy character . . . Set your
> minds, then, on endorsing by your conduct the fact
> that God has called and chosen you. If you go along the
> lines I have indicated . . . , there is no reason why
> you should stumble, . . . [5]

It was John who gave me the key to handling all my relationships:

> . . . if we love each other, God does actually live with-
> in us, and His love grows in us towards perfection.
> And the guarantee of our living in Him and His living
> in us is the share of His own Spirit which He gives us
> . . . God is love and the man whose life is lived in love
> does, in fact, live in God, and God does, in fact, live in
> him . . . Love contains no fear—indeed

fully-developed love expels every particle of fear . . .[6]

How shall we believers deal with each other? Paul summed it up in the first chapter of Ephesians: "The Messiah came to the Gentiles as well as the Jews to reconcile them both to God the Father; each of them has been selected and adopted into God's family in exactly the same way; each of them is a joint heir with Jesus and, therefore, they are joint heirs with one another."

As a result of all my months of study, prayer and experience, I came to this position.

I am a Jew. I was born a Jew, and I will die a Jew. Even if it were possible for me to reject my Jewish identity and heritage, I would never do so. I am a Jew by birth and by desire.

As a matter of fact, I am so comfortable and so secure in my Jewish identity that I am not threatened by the fears and anxieties of some who would question it. My Jewishness was not conferred upon me by public opinion or by government edict. It was not given to me by men, and it cannot be taken away from me by men.

As a Jew, I am even more sensitive to the teachings of Jesus, who was born a Jew, lived as a Jew, chose other Jews as His disciples and loved the Jewish people. As His disciple today, I know that He is more concerned about the attitudes of our hearts than of the actions we perform. This knowledge permits me to have the peace I need to lay all of these issues before Him, to cast my cares upon Him as I yield to the very Spirit of God and follow after peace, love and joy.

In my relations with other believers, Jews or Gentiles, I am to follow after the peace that passes understanding as I seek the wisdom which comes from above. I am to avoid wrath and anger and striving on my own as the love nature of God becomes more manifest in me.

In my relations with members of my family and friends I

am to remain consistent, never turning my back on my heritage, on my ancestry, on Israel or upon them.

But there is a caveat in all of this. I must allow nothing to become a stumbling block for me. Should a desire well up within me to please others—especially if it means compromising the Word of God—I am in serious danger. The Word tells us that many will stumble at the stumbling stone. Jesus is the stumbling stone. We who believe are told not to tarry but to press on and to follow Him. As we do so, the peace that passes understanding confirms the Word of God.

The history of the last 2,000 years has focused our attention upon man's inhumanity to man. In the process the issue became self-preservation. It was critical that we Jews protect ourselves from those who would destroy the Jewish people. It still is. But the God who formed us and chose us and held out His hands to us and covenanted with us, has not set out to destroy us. Nor have those who were true believers been guilty of the atrocities which took place.

How do I explain the last 2,000 years? I cannot. But I know this: the real issue is not the secular history of this period. Nor is it the "Jewishness" of those who believe. The issue is Jesus. Is He or is He not God's anointed? Is He who He says He is? Is He or is He not the Messiah?

I thank God that His Word is true and that it has set me free. I praise God that I may read the old covenant and the new covenant and recognize the one Author. I rejoice that the warnings of Deuteronomy have become clear to me and that I have been able to choose life. I soar in my spirit as I press on toward the mark of His high calling in my life.

God is! The God of Abraham, Isaac and Jacob is. The Messiah is. Jesus is the Messiah. Oh, the freedom that wells up in me. I need not dance to the drumbeats of "custom" or of "tradition" or of "old hatred" or of "fear." *My God reigns!* And *in Him* I live and move and have my being.

How do I contain the power and the reality of these truths? They pour from every fibre of my being. This is the good news that awaits all who seek to find and know God!

16

Since Then

An explosion took place in my life. My eyes saw. My ears heard. My horizons expanded. My perceptions increased. My joy reached new heights. And I developed a voracious appetite for God's Word.

As people throughout the greater Washington, D.C., area learned about what was happening to Ethel and to me, invitations came in for each of us to share our excitement. In time, we were invited to begin teaching. Though less than qualified initially, I recognized that the discipline of having to prepare to teach others on a regular basis would be an enormous opportunity for me to learn. It would force me to study the Word. It was a great challenge, and I accepted it.

Our first assignment was in a congregation in Washington, D.C. Here, Ethel and I were asked to teach the career class made up of young adults who were starting out in professional life. Our class started with about 24 young people, soon grew to more than 75 of all ages. When I probed the students about those areas where they needed help, more than 80 confidential replies came to me. Their problems included terrible feelings of unworthiness, loneliness, unforgiveness of self and of others, relationship problems with parents and peers, self-consciousness, anxiety about dating, love, sex, marriage and choosing careers.

Our challenge was to search the Scriptures and to present Biblical principles to some 75 people by which they could live their lives with freedom and power.

Next came a Bible study in our home. Originally I invited 24 believers to the Bible study: 12 Jews and 12 Gentiles. I wanted to see the power of God's Word operate within this mixed group. Though we ended up with more Gentile than Jewish believers, new relationships were formed and lives were changed during these Wednesday evenings in our home. A fantastic experience!

Then an even greater spiritual responsibility beckoned: to be a real shepherd to these people. I knew that I loved people, that I was a good father and a good teacher. But when asked when I would enter the ministry, I experienced sudden inner conflict. It was the desire of my heart, but I was reluctant to promote myself. To double-check what was happening within me, I visited with six mature pastors I knew in the Washington, D.C., and Baltimore areas and asked them if they had any perception of God's call upon my life.

To my joy, each of them confirmed the call. One even told me that he had known about it for more than a year and was wondering when I would recognize it.

Then one day a friend telephoned me from San Francisco. After an exchange of pleasantries, he came to the point. "Stan, I want to ask you a question. What are you going to do with the rest of your life?"

A big question to try and answer on a coast-to-coast call.

In an hour and a half conversation, he pinpointed these recommendations: take a sabbatical from your business; go to a good Bible school for a year or so; don't try to go through seminary, you don't need it; at the Bible school learn of God and come back prepared to minister to the needs of the people God will send to you.

These suggestions made my spirit soar. I knew I needed

more schooling in God's Word before I could truly minister to the spiritual needs of people.

But what to do about my business? After 25 years, it was in excellent shape, and I had hundreds of important client relationships. Could I leave the business for a year? Would Jenny stay to look after my clients?

It amazed me how quickly everything fell into place. First, Ethel responded positively. Then Jenny agreed to handle my clients for a year. Our home sold on July 30, 1979, and we left for Bible school three weeks later.

Leaving Ann who had just graduated from art school, was the hardest part. "I've heard everything now," she told us with a smile. "Usually kids leave parents to go to college, but I've never heard of parents leaving kids to go to Bible School!"

After living in large homes for most of our married lives, Ethel and I suddenly found ourselves adjusting to a small, two-bedroom apartment with cheap rented furniture. The transition would have been ludicrous had we not been so happy. In many ways this opportunity to start life all over again with Ethel was one of the greatest experiences of my life. It was not only a time for new beginnings in the Lord's work but also a time for new discoveries about each other.

Nine months later, May 28, 1980, we were back in Washington. I re-entered my insurance office. Sixteen days later I also became the spiritual leader of the Living Word Fellowship in Bethesda, Maryland. This is an open, inter-denominational fellowship made up of Jewish and Gentile believers.

Our primary emphasis, however, is in helping the new creations God brings to our fellowship to learn that they are complete in the Messiah; to enable them to understand the reality of what has happened in their lives. They are being set free of bondage and the philosophies of men. They are not involved in seeking to please men. They are involved in looking to the Lord to perform His Word. The miracle of God's love and His grace is operational in their lives. They can never again be what they once were. They are being transformed before our very eyes. And the joy which cannot be explained fills their hearts despite all trials and testings.

One of the interesting aspects of our ministry is the way Ethel and I have been able to bring the Jewish perspective through the Scriptures. Most people, Jews and Gentiles alike, don't fully appreciate the Jewishness of the first 15 chapters of Acts. Nor have they ever heard Ephesians introduced from a Jewish point of view. Most of the Gentiles have never attended a Passover Seder, and when I conduct an abbreviated Seder each year, they are thrilled by the insight they receive. The joy of Rosh Hashanah and solemnity of Yom Kippur are shared with the congregation as we show the messianic implications of each.

At Purim, Ethel will teach the book of Esther and make hundreds of "hummin tashen" for the people. (These are the triangular pastries many Jewish people make at this holiday season.) For Channukah, the Festival of Lights, Ethel will bring hundreds of latkes (potato pancakes which are eaten during this holiday season with sour cream and applesauce). While we have not felt led to follow any traditional Jewish form in our worship service, the richness of our heritage flows from us as we focus on the God of our fathers and worship Him in Spirit and in Truth.

Our family has never been more fulfilled as every one of us knows the truth about Jesus and has acted upon that truth. Ann is working as a make-up artist and doing lithography as she can. Judy was married on April 15, 1978, to John Mangat-Rai and on April 17, 1979, presented us with our very own first grandchild: beautiful, charming, talented, lovely Jennifer.

I continue to try to improve my relationships with the members of my family who are still living. One brother is very supportive of my work. While my other brother and sisters know a little about our new lives, we have not felt free to fully share everything with them, preferring to concentrate on what unites us rather than what divides us. I understand their concern and will be patient, for I love them dearly.

With a clarity that I never thought would be possible, I know who I am and what I am to do. I thrill at the challenge and responsibility of leading and feeding God's people.

Having made our decision from deep within our hearts, Ethel and I say to Jew and Gentile alike—*Shalom*: as we wish you freedom from all fears and moral conflicts; freedom from strife and from stress; good health and prosperity with all of your personal and spiritual needs met as you enjoy God's rest.

A Look at Some Prophecies

Recent studies by Biblical scholars indicate that there are 456 prophecies concerning the Messiah. What are the laws of probability on the fulfillment of these prophecies? Peter Stoner wrote an article on this in *Science Speaks* (Moody Press 1963) in which he considered these eight prophecies:

1. The place of the Messiah's birth;
2. His being preceded by a messenger;
3. How He was to enter Jerusalem;
4. His betrayal by a friend;
5. He would be betrayed for 30 pieces of silver;
6. The money would be thrown in God's house;
7. He would be mute before His accusers;
8. He would be crucified.

Stoner reported that by using the modern science of probability in reference to these eight prophecies, "we find that the chance that any man might have lived down to the present time and fulfilled all eight prophecies is one in ten to the 17th power. This would be 1 in 100,000,000,000,000,-000. In order to help us comprehend this we take 10 to the 17th power in silver dollars and lay them down on the face of Texas. They will cover the state two feet deep. Now mark one of these silver dollars and stir the whole mass thoroughly, all over the state. Blindfold a man and tell him that he can travel as far as he wishes, but he must pick up one silver dollar and say that this is the right one. What chance would he have of getting the right one? Just the same chance that the prophets would have had of writing these eight prophecies and having them all come true in any one man, from their day to the present time, providing they wrote them in their own wisdom."

What then is the probability of one man fulfilling each and every one of the 41 prophecies listed below? Astronomical! And what chance would there be of fulfilling the 456 prophecies the Old Testament contains? Beyond comprehension.

By way of summary, I will once again refer to the prophecy contained in Daniel 9:26. Here we are told that the city and the sanctuary will be destroyed by the prince who shall come *after the Messiah has been cut off*.

This occurred in A.D. 70 when the Temple was destroyed by Titus and his legions. Recall with me that genealogy was of critical importance in Israel and in Jewish life. Remember that the genealogies were maintained in the Temple. When the Temple was destroyed the genealogies were also destroyed. With their destruction, it would never again be possible for anyone to prove that any man proclaiming himself as the Messiah could belong to the House of David. And this was a critical proof needed to establish that he was the Messiah. The Messiah had to be of the seed of Abraham, the Son of Isaac, the Son of Jacob, of the Tribe of Judah, of the Family of Jesse, and of the House of David.

If no one could ever establish his ancestry, no Messiah could ever be proved. This reasoning puts all Jews in a very uncomfortable position: either the prophecies concerning the Messiah are incorrect and thereby false; and the entire concept of a Messiah in Jewish life is nothing more than a myth; and the Bible is nothing more than a story book of the Jewish people; or the Messiah came before the Temple was destroyed.

The following 41 prophecies are selected from *Evidence that Demands a Verdict* by Josh McDowell.

PROPHECY	FULFILLMENT
Son of God "I will surely tell of the decree of the Lord: He said to me, 'Thou art My Son, this day I have begotten Thee. Psalms 2:7. See also: I Chronicles 17:11-14; II Samuel 7:12-16	". . . and behold a voice out of the heavens, saying, 'This is My beloved Son, in whom I am well pleased." Matthew 3:17.
Seed of Abraham "And in your descendants all the nations of the earth shall be blessed, because you have obeyed My voice." Genesis 22:18	"The book of the genealogy of Jesus, the Messiah, the Son of David, the Son of Abraham." Matthew 1:1
Son of Isaac "But God said to Abraham . . . through Isaac your descendants shall be named. Genesis 21:12	"Jesus . . . the son of Isaac . . ." Luke 3:23,24

Son of Jacob

"I see him, but now now; I
behold him, but not near; A
star shall come forth from
Jacob, and a scepter shall rise
from Israel, and shall crush
through the forehead of Moab,
and tear down all the sons of
Sheth."
Numbers 24:17

"Jesus . . . the son of
Jacob . . ."
Luke 3:23,24

Tribe of Judah

"The scepter shall not depart
from Judah, nor the ruler's
staff from between his feet,
Until Shiloh comes, And to
him shall be the obedience of
the peoples."
Genesis 40:10

"Jesus, . . . the son of Judah
. . ."
Luke 3:23,33

Family Line of Jesse

"Then a shoot will spring from
the stem of Jesse, And a branch
from his roots will bear fruit."
Isaiah 11:1

"Jesus, the son of
Jesse . . ."
Luke 3:23,32

House of David

"Behold, the days are coming,
declares the Lord, when I shall
raise up for David a righteous
branch; And he will reign as
King and act wisely, And do
justice and righteousness in
the land."
Jeremiah 23:5

"Jesus, the son of
David . . ."
Luke 3:23,31.

His pre-existence
"But as for you, Bethlehem Ephratah, Too little to be among the clans of Judah, From you One will go forth for Me to be ruler in Israel. His goings forth are from long ago, From the days of eternity."
Micah 5:2

"And He is before all things, and in Him, all things hold together."
Collosians 1:17

He shall be called Lord
"The Lord said to my Lord; 'Sit at my right hand, until I make thine enemies a footstool for thy feet' "
Psalms 110:1

"For today in the city of David, there has been born to you a Savior, who is Messiah the Lord."
Luke 2:11

He shall be a prophet
"I will raise them up a Prophet from among their brethern like you, and will put My words in his mouth, and he shall speak unto them all that I shall command him.
Deuteronomy 18:18

"And the multitudes were saying, 'This is the prophet Jesus, from Nazareth in Galilee.' "
Matthew 21:11

He shall be a priest
"The Lord has sworn and will not change His mind, 'Thou art a priest forever according to the order of Malchizedek.' "
Psalms 110:4

"Therefore, holy brethren, partakers of a heavenly calling, consider Jesus, the Apostle and High Priest of our confession."
Hebrews 3:1

He shall be a judge
"For the Lord is our judge, The Lord is our lawgiver, The Lord is our king; He will save us. . ."
Isaiah 33:22

"I can do nothing on my own initiative, as I hear, I judge and My judgement is just, because I do not seek My own will be the will of Him who sent me."
John 5:30

He shall be a King
"But as for Me, I have installed My King upon Zion, My holy mountain."
Psalms 2:6

"And they put above His head the charge against Him which read, 'This is Jesus the King of the Jews' "
Matthew 27:37

He shall be anointed of the Holy Spirit
"And the Spirit of the Lord will rest on Him, the spirit of wisdom and understanding, The spirit of counsel and strength. The spirit of knowledge and the fear of the Lord."
Isaiah 11:2

"And after being baptized, Jesus went up immediately from the water; and behold, the heavens were opened, and He saw the Spirit of God descending as a dove, and coming upon Him; and behold a voice out of the heavens, saying, 'This is My beloved Son, in whom I am well pleased.' "
Matthew 3:16-17

He will perform miracles:
"Then the eyes of the blind will be opened, And the ears of the deaf will be unstopped, Then the lame will leap like a deer, And the tongue of the dumb will shout for joy."
Isaiah 35:5,6a

"And Jesus was going about all the cities and the villages teaching in their synagogues and proclaiming the gospel of the kingdom, and healing every kind of disease and every kind of sickness."
Matthew 9:35

He will teach parables:
"I will open my mouth in a parable; I will utter dark sayings of old."
Psalm 78:2

"All these things Jesus spoke to the multitudes in parables, and He was not talking to them without a parable."
Matthew 13:34

He would be betrayed by a friend:
"Even my close friend, in whom I trusted, who ate my bread, has lifted up his heel against me."
Psalms 41:9

" . . . Judas Iscariot, the one who betrayed Him."
Matthew 10:4

He would be sold for 30 pieces of silver:
"And I said to them, 'if it is good in your sight, give me my wages; but if not, never mind!' So they weighed out thirty shekels of silver as my wages."
Zechariah 11:12

" . . . 'What are you willing to give me to deliver Him up to you?' And they weighed out to him thirty pieces of silver."
Matthew 26:15

The money would be thrown in God's house:
" . . . So I took the thirty shekels of silver and threw them to the potter in the house of the Lord."
Zechariah 11:13b

"And he threw the pieces of silver into the sanctuary and departed . . ."
Matthew 27:5a

He would be forsaken by His disciples:
". . . Strike the Shepherd that the sheep may be scattered . . ."
Zechariah 13:7

"And they all left Him and fled."
Mark 14:50

He would be accused by false witnesses:
"Malicious witnesses rise up; they ask me of things that I do not know."
Psalm 35:11

"Now the chief priests and the whole council kept trying to obtain false testimony against Jesus, in order that they might put Him to death; and they did not find it, even though many false witnesses came forward."
Matthew 26:59-61

He would not respond to His accusers:
"He was oppressed and He was afflicted, Yet He did not open His mouth."
Isaiah 53:7

"And while He was being accused by the chief priests and elders, He made no answer."
Matthew 27:12-19

He would be wounded and bruised:
"But He was wounded for our transgressions, He was bruised for our inquities. The chastisement of our peace was upon Him, and with His stripes we are healed."
Isaiah 53:5

"Then he released Barabbas for them; but Jesus he scourged and delivered over to be crucified."
Matthew 27:26

He would be smitten and split upon:

"I gave My back to those who strike me, And My cheeks to those who pluck out the beard; I did not cover My face from humiliation and spitting."
Isaiah 50:6

"Then they spat in His face and beat Him with their fists and others slapped Him."
Matthew 26:67

He would be mocked:

"All they that see me laugh me to scorn: they shoot out the lip, they shake the head, saying, He trusted on the Lord that He would deliver Him: let Him deliver Him seeing He delighted in Him."
Psalms 22:2-8

"And after they had mocked Him, they took His robe off and put His garments on Him, and led Him away to crucify Him."
Matthew 27:31

His hands and feet would be pierced:

"They pierced my hands and my feet."
Psalms 22:16

"And when they came to the place called The Skull, there they crucified Him . . . "
Luke 23:33

He made intercession for His persecutors:

" . . . yet He Himself bore the sins of many, and interceded for the transgressors."
Isaiah 53:12

"Father forgive them, for they do not know what they are doing."
Luke 23:34

*He would be hated by His own
people:*
"He was despised and
forsaken of men, a man of
sorrows, and acquainted with
grief; And like one from whom
men hide their face. He was
despised, and we did not
esteem Him."
Isaiah 53:3

"For not even His brothers
were believing in Him. Not one
of the rulers or Pharisees has
believed in Him, has he?"
John 7:5,48.

He would be hated without a cause:
"Those who hate me without a
cause are more than the hairs
of my
head . . ."
Psalms 69:4

"But they have done this in
order that the word may be fulfilled that is written in their
Law, 'They hated Me without a
cause.' "
John 15:25

His friends would stand afar off:
"My loved ones and my
friends stand aloof from my
plague: And my kinsmen
stand afar off."
Psalm 38:11

"And all His acquaintances
and the women who accompa-
nied Him from Galilee, were
standing at a distance, seeing
these things."
Luke 23:49

People shook their heads at Him:
"I also have become a reproach
to them; When they see me,
they wag their head."
Psalms 109:25

"And those who were passing
by were hurling abuse at Him,
wagging their heads."
Matthew 27:39

*They divided His garments and
cast lots for them.*

"They divided my garments
among them, And for my
clothing they cast lots."
Psalm 22:18

"The soldiers therefore, when
they had crucified Jesus, took
His outer garments and made
four parts, a part to every soldier and also the tunic; now the
tunic was seamless, woven in
one piece. They said: "Let us
not tear it, but cast lots for it,
to decide whose it shall
be . . ."
John 19:23,24

He was to suffer thirst:

" . . . And for my thirst they
gave me vinegar to drink."
Psalms 69:21

"After this, Jesus . . . said, 'I
am thirsty'."

*They offered him gall and vinegar
to drink:*

"They also gave me gall for my
food, and for my thirst they
gave me vinegar to drink."
Psalms 69:21

"They gave Him wine to drink
mingled with gall; and after
tasting it, He was unwilling to
drink."
Matthew 27:34

He cried aloud:

"My God, My God, why hast
thou forsaken me?"
Psalms 22:1

"And about the ninth hour,
Jesus cried out with a loud
voice, saying, 'Eli, Eli, Lama
Sabachthani,' that is, 'My God,
my God, why hast thou forsaken me?"
Matthew 27:46

He committed His Spirit:
"Into thy hands I commit my
spirit."
Psalm 31:5

"And Jesus, crying out with a
loud voice, said, 'Father, into
thy hands I commit My Spirit."
Luke 23:46

His bones were not broken:
"He keeps all His bones, not
one of them is broken."
Psalms 34:20

" . . . but coming to Jesus,
when they saw that He was
already dead, they did not
break His legs."
John 19:33

His heart was broken:
"My heart is like wax, it is
melted within me."
Psalms 22:14

" . . . but one of the soldiers
pierced His side with a spear,
and immediately there came
out blood and water."
John 19:34

His side was pierced:
" . . . they will look on Me
whom they have pierced."
Zechariah 12:10

" . . . but one of the soldiers
pierced His side with a spear."
John 19:34

And darkness came over the land:
" 'And it will come about in
that day' declares the Lord
God, 'that I shall make the sun
go down at noon and make the
earth dark in broad daylight
. . .' "
Amos 8:9

"Now from the sixth hour
darkness fell upon all the land
until the ninth hour."
Matthew 27:45

He was buried in a rich man's tomb:

"His grave was assigned to be with wicked men, Yet with a rich man in His death."
Isaiah 53:9

" . . . there came a rich man from Arimathea, named Joseph . . . and asked for the body of Jesus . . . and Joseph took the body and wrapped it in a clean linen cloth, and laid it in his own new tomb.".
Matthew 27:57-60

Scripture References

Chapter Three:
1. Deut 6:8; 11:18 (ASV)

Chapter Four:
1. Deut 6:4 (ASV)
2. Matthew 4:10 (ASV)
3. Matthew 15:24 (ASV)

Chapter Six:
1. Daniel 9:24,25,26

Chapter Seven:
1. Luke 7:22

Chapter Eight:
1. John 5:45,46
2. Genesis 12:1-3
3. Genesis 13:14,15
4. Genesis 17:1,2a
5. Genesis 17:3b-6a
6. Genesis 17:10,11
7. Exodus 6:2,3a
8. Exodus 6:4a
9. Exodus 6:5,6
10. Exodus 24:3,7,8
11. Ezra 10:10b,11

Chapter Nine:
1. Acts 10:11-16
2. Acts 10:44 RSV

Chapter Ten:
1. Luke 21:20-24 (ASV)

Chapter Fifteen:
1. Matthew 5:11
2. Matthew 10:22
3. Luke 18:29-30
4. I Peter 4:7,8 (Phillips)
5. II Peter 3:11 and 1:10 (Phillips)
6. I John 4:12,16,18

Bibliography

1. Bruce, F. F. THE SPREADING FLAME, Grand Rapids, Ml. Wm. B. Eerdmans Publishing Co., 1973.
2. Dimont, Max I. JEWS, GOD AND HISTORY, New York. Simon & Shuster, 1961.
3. Eban, Abba MY PEOPLE, New York. Behrain House, Inc. 1968
4. Edersheim, Alfred THE LIFE AND TIMES OF JESUS THE MESSIAH, Grand Rapids, Ml. Eerdmans Publishing Co.
5. Ellison, J. L. THE MYSTERY OF ISRAEL, Grand Rapids, Ml. Eerdman's Publishing Co., 1966.
6. Fruchtenbaum, Arnold G. HEBREW CHRISTIANITY: IT'S THEOLOGY, HISTORY AND PHILOSOPHY, Washington, D.C. Canon Press, 1974.
7. Harkavy, Alexander THE HOLY SCRIPTURES, New York. Hebrew Publishing Company, 1963.
8. Klausner, Joseph THE MESSIANIC IDEA IN ISRAEL, New York. MacMillan, 1955.
9. Latourette, Kenneth Scott A HISTORY OF CHRISTIANITY, New York. Harper and Brothers, 1953.
10. Latourette, Kenneth Scott. A HISTORY OF THE EXPANSION OF CHRISTIANITY, Vol. 1, "The First Five Centuries", Grand Rapids, Ml. Zondervan Publishing Company, 1970.
11. McDowell, Josh EVIDENCE THAT DEMANDS A VERDICT, Arrowhead Springs, CA. Campus Crusade for Christ International, 1972.
12. Phillips, J. B. THE NEW TESTAMENT IN MODERN ENGLISH, New York. MacMillan Publishing Co., Inc., 1958.
13. Sachar, Abram Leon A HISTORY OF THE JEWS, New York. Alfred A. Knopf, 1965.
14. Scholem, Gershon THE MESSIANIC IDEA IN JUDAISM, New York. Shoken Books, 1971.
15. THE NEW TESTAMENT WITH OLD TESTAMENT REFERENCES, Philadelphia, PA. Million Testaments Campaign.

We want to hear from you. Please send your
comments about this book to us in care of the
address below. Thank you.

ZONDERVAN™

GRAND RAPIDS, MICHIGAN 49530 USA

WWW.ZONDERVAN.COM